COMPETENT
MINISTRY

COMPETENT MINISTRY

A Guide
to
Effective
Continuing
Education

MARK A. ROUCH

ABINGDON PRESS

Nashville   New York

COMPETENT MINISTRY

Copyright © 1974 by Abingdon Press

Library of Congress Cataloging in Publication Data

ROUCH, MARK A   1925-   Competent ministry.
    Competent ministry.
    Bibliography: p.
    1. Clergy—Post-ordination training. I. Title.
BV4165.R66   207'.1   73-22309

ISBN 0-687-09318-X

MANUFACTURED BY THE PARTHENON PRESS AT
NASHVILLE, TENNESSEE, UNITED STATES OF AMERICA

To Phyllis, Catherine,
and Jordan

CONTENTS

PREFACE

This is a book about continuing education for ministry. It is designed as a tool for pastors, Christian educators, and other professional church leaders who want to engage in continuing education with increased effectiveness.

I am convinced that growing numbers of our profession believe that continuing education is essential to an authentic and effective ministry. Thousands of us participate each year in programs, seminars, and study groups which are, or claim to be, continuing education. Thousands more want to become involved but have not known exactly how to get underway. There is thus a widespread need for help both in knowing how to become involved and how to make our continuing education productive. This book is designed to offer such help. It will not provide all the help needed; no single resource can. It does, however, supply one needed tool and at numerous places points to other resources, material and personal.

For eight years now, my working life has been devoted almost entirely to continuing education for ministry. These have been exciting years in watching continuing education become a significant movement in the American church—Protestant and Roman

Catholic. I have had opportunity to become acquainted with the broad and diversified range of resoures at our disposal both in the church and outside it. I have discussed continuing education with thousands of pastors, local church educators, and other professional leaders. I have benefited from the counsel of those who plan programs for and with them, including colleagues in the national continuing education offices of other denominations. In this book I have attempted to bring together the learnings of these years in a way that will be useful to all those who are engaged or want to become engaged in this enterprise. I have even hoped that the book might lure some into continuing education who have not until now sensed its importance.

This book is also about growing competence in ministry. Competence is the primary outcome of effective continuing education. When it is not, something is amiss. All genuine education has intrinsic values. The person who has not experienced the sheer joy of learning has missed one of life's treasures. But continuing education for ministry, as for all professions, is highly instrumental. It is an instrument to help us become competent. It is, in fact, the primary instrument. Few of us have fully appropriated continuing education as a taproot of growing competence. That this book will help that happen is my strong hope.

As you have already sensed, I have studiously avoided writing only for pastors. Other professional leaders have a key role in the church, and continuing education is fully as crucial for them as for pastors. In fact much continuing education will be most effective when a variety of professional leaders are involved collegially.

Chapter 1 defines continuing education, not in terms of a final definition for a subject hard to pin down, but rather, to provide a provisional definition which will serve as a common reference point as we proceed.

Chapter 2 sets continuing education in the matrix of lifelong learning, which I see primarily as an attitude of openness to life. Chapter 3 deals with the relationship between continuing education and competence, including the importance of the desire for competence as a motivation for learning.

Chapters 4 and 5 are, in a sense, the heart of the book. Four suggests the techniques and methods for planning and carrying out your own continuing education program. Chapter 5 looks at the resources available. The remaining chapters address the central problems, issues, concerns which affect and can enrich continuing education.

Throughout I refer to specific program agencies, programs, periodicals, and other helps. In a movement so young and in a day of such rapid change, some of these may be nonexistent even before this book is in print. Without such specificity, however, the book's usefulness as a guide would be diminished. Many of the resources mentioned, however, are well established, and the text refers at many points to agencies from which up-to-date specific information can be obtained.

I hope that women, as well as men, will find this book a useful guide. Writing it, however, has heightened the awareness of my limitations as a man in understanding the situation of women in a male-dominated culture and profession. If the book proves useful to women in continuing education, it will be due, to a great extent, to the ideas and suggestions of those women with whom I have discussed its concerns. I am especially indebted to Betty Strathman Pagett for information concerning continuing education resources for women in chapter 5.

Space flight is now symbolic of invention and exploration as group achievements. Authors, I suppose, have always known that about their books. While I take full responsibility for what is said in this particular "exploration," I know full well that many persons have made it possible.

My family, first, from whom I have borrowed many hours and days and who have always encouraged me in the project.

Second, my secretary, Mrs. Ruth Walker, who has willingly gone far beyond the line of duty in typing and retyping and retyping the manuscript. Her gentle reminders and suggestions have been invaluable.

To no person do I owe more for my understanding of continuing education than Dr. Connolly Gamble, Director of Continuing Education at Union Theological Seminary, Richmond, and Executive Secretary of the Society for the Advancement of Continuing Education for Ministry. When I began my work eight years ago, Dr. Gamble was and has remained the "dean" of the continuing education for ministry movement. He more than any other urged me to rethink my understanding of continuing education, resulting finally in the definition which I propose in this book. From his broad knowledge of the movement and keen insight I continue to learn.

Were it possible to list the many others to whom I am indebted, I would name many colleagues in several primary groups: the staff of the United Methodist Board of Higher Education and Ministry and its predecessor agencies with whom I have worked these eight years. Among these colleagues, I feel a special and profound debt to Dr. Myron F. Wicke, former General Secretary of the Division of Higher Education. The other denominational executives, past and present, who comprise the Ecumenical Continuing Education Team. Those with responsibility for continuing education leadership in the seminaries and annual conferences of United Methodism. Finally, associates in the Society for the Advancement of Continuing Education for Ministry.

Chapter I

CONTINUING EDUCATION: WHAT IS IT?

He walked into the group a half hour late. The pain was severe, and he had not been sure that he could share it with anyone else; he had almost stayed home. Last night the pastor-parish relations committee had told him that his ministry did not fit their needs. Next week they would ask the district superintendent to find them someone else. He had known of the dissatisfaction but thought it had begun to subside. The last two years had not been easy. After Martha's miscarriage the next baby had been healthy enough, but he usually felt guilty that he spent so little time with them. In seminary he'd always been at the center of student government affairs, but now he felt virtually powerless in his annual conference. But underlying it all was a sense that he was not prepared for this ingrown, rural parish to which he had been sent.

If he had not been meeting with these six other young pastors for a year now he could not have faced them this morning. But as they had worked together on increasing their competence in ministry, trust had gradually built, trust that he had not experienced in any other group. With trust had come support. It had helped for Fred to be there. An older, more experienced pastor whom they had invited to meet with them, he had been a strong understanding friend and they had often profited from his experience.

For two hours he unloaded his feelings. At noon they decided to meet within one week instead of the usual two; they knew that an urgent agenda had been cut out for them.

She opened the monthly packet containing *Thesis Theological Cassettes.* Margaret Mead's name caught her eye. Without listening to the others she advanced the tape to that lecture. Fascinated by the discussion which put contemporary society's problems in the long view of history, she thought of the adult class she had been working with on Sunday mornings. The next week they listened to the tape and spent the following Sunday discussing it. It was one of their liveliest episodes.

He had read *I'm OK, You're OK*—who hadn't. Intrigued, he had read again *Games People Play.* Bill had told him of the skillful Transactional Analysis training at a California institute. With eleven other professionals, most of them unrelated to the church, he had taken eight days of Transactional Analysis training. Costly, but worth it. He now saw things about himself which he had not seen before. Within a month after returning he had read *What Do You Say After You Say Hello?* and *Born Free.*

The parish consultation had gone well. Gradually, healing processes had begun to work. A group study of reconciliation in the New Testament had had more meaning—so they said— than any they could remember. He thought so too. He could not help reflecting on his involvement with them as a colearner; some of the old artificial deference to him as pastor was gone. Perhaps, he thought, it was because lately they had been talking to one another more honestly.

His mind went back to Thursday night's consultation session. The conversation had been strained at first, but easier as it progressed. (He admired their consultant's communication skills.) Alex had told him that a feeling had gradually spread through the congregation that his preaching was becoming superficial. But Jean had pointed to their discovery of the administrative load they expected him to carry; little wonder he lacked time for sermon preparation. The outcome had been encouraging. They had suggested that he take more time for study and had agreed that he would begin to look for a program on preaching designed especially for his needs—and theirs. This would be the right occasion, Alex had said, to put financial support and time allowance for continuing education into the budget and call agreement.

He had not expected a discussion of theology at 2:00 A.M. In fact, this entire program had surprised him. All evening they had been in contact with the city's night people; their last stop, a gay bar. Now back at the seminary, they were discussing with a young theologian questions which the evening had raised: What is a human being? Does God liberate—really? What is the church? Can it minister to outcasts? The discussion was heated and intense. He could not remember when theology had been so alive.

Two weeks ago, he thought, they could not have managed this much conflict. When they arrived their defenses were up. They had been afraid of one another. He himself had often felt angry; most of these middle-class white ministers had little idea of what it means to be black. The human relations training during the first week had helped. Tonight he not only sensed that they had begun to mold a community which could handle conflict, but he also saw the faint possibility of their renewal in ministry. It would all depend.

WHAT IS IT—REALLY?

Each of these episodes is continuing education. Yet none of them is. By exploring this apparent contradiction, I believe we can arrive at a useful definition of a term hard to define.

Each episode, then, *is* continuing education. Continuing education can occur in many different settings, using a variety of methods and resources. Not for a minute would I claim that every experience which pretends to be educational actually is. We waste hours, dollars, psychic energy in "educational" events which change us only slightly or not at all.

I am also uneasy, however, with educational dogmatism. Learning occurs in far too many settings with far too many methods for me to be convinced that there is only one way or one setting. Testimony to the contrary is overwhelming.

But the very fact of variety creates problems for us. What kind of program is right for me—now? Which claim shall I believe? Is it better to use a resource at home or travel five hundred miles for a ten-day program? Some of us, without answering such questions have plunged in wherever the most attractive or convenient opportunity appeared; some of us have hesitated quite bewildered.

I hope that this book will help you make effective choices in the midst of this diversity. However, my primary concern at the moment is simply to say that continuing education can occur in many diverse places and ways.

Yet *none* of the episodes is continuing education. Not singly, or even in series are they continuing education in its fullest sense. To think that they are is a major pitfall into which many of us have stumbled. Continuing education is a process; all education is. It contains distinct episodes and events such as those I have described. But the word "continuing" is more important than many of us have allowed. *Continuing* education is a long-term—career-long or lifelong—process with distinct events and episodes, linked together by strong continuing themes.

Thus, the cases we described, and many more like them, may be episodes in a continuing process. As part of this process, they *are* continuing education. As isolated events, unrelated to the larger process, they *are not*—at least not in a productive sense. This is how I define it: *Continuing education is an individual's personally designed learning program which begins when basic formal education ends and continues throughout a career and beyond. An unfolding process, it links together personal study and reflection and participation in organized group events.*

This is a working definition. It says what I mean by continuing education in the discussions which follow. More important, I intend it as a starting point or occasion for rethinking as you define continuing education for yourself. The definition indicates that I view continuing education as each individual's *own* program of learning. Accordingly, I believe that the definition of continuing education for you must be one which you adopt for yourself. Thus, in no sense do I intend this definition as final. It is the one at which I have arrived for the time being; the one I use in this book; and one which I hope will be useful to you as you formulate your own.[1]

In this definition I have used *designed, program, organized.* I view continuing education as the more formal or planned part of our total learning experience. Life's learning is vast—or ought to be. We learn more, I suspect, in completely informal unplanned ways than in those more formal and planned. The informal unplanned part of learning I choose to call "lifelong learning" (cf. chapter 2). The choice to call only the more formal and planned experiences "continuing education" is somewhat pragmatic. I have found it more manageable to think and write about this more limited group of learning experiences. If your mind works differently, well and good.

By "basic formal education" I refer to the basic education which qualifies one through ordination or certification to begin professional practice. Degree programs afterward are part of continuing education, especially the new doctor of ministry

[1] During the early years of the continuing education movement definitions were premature. Some would claim that they still are. I believe, however, that the time has come to say what we mean by continuing education. In stating the above definition I realize that there are others with equal validity. As definitions are proposed, dialogue will produce more adequate definitions than any one of us could reach alone.

17

degrees. You will notice that I have not referred to degree programs in relation to basic education. I recognize that most professionals have qualified for practice through degree programs. Some of you will have qualified in other ways, such as through what United Methodists call the "course of study." Continuing education is fully as appropriate and necessary for you as for those who have graduated from seminary. In fact, you may have a head start since your basic studies will probably have been done as in-service training.

Continuing education may continue long into retirement—as may a career. In this book we shall look only at the years up to retirement and limit the discussion of continuing education accordingly.

So much for a brief exegesis of the definition.

At the outset we should realize the radical shift which this definition may require if we take it seriously.

First, it places the primary responsibility for continuing education on each of us—not someone else. The organization of the plan, its revision, the search for resources, and the decision to use them—these become our own primary responsibility. But that is quite different from the conditioning of our school years. Then someone else always had a large degree of responsibility. As our education proceeded we were free to take more and more of the responsibility, and if we did not our education was indeed impoverished. But still someone else provided the institution; someone else had primary responsibility for the curriculum; someone else planned the courses.

But now the situation is reversed. Others may enter into the planning. (If, in fact, they do not we are again impoverished.) Many resources are available. But now the primary responsibility is our own—no one else's.

Second, it requires that we break out of the "classroom concept" of education. As children, we were given to believe that learning *really* began when we went to school. The vast learnings of preschool days—probably more rapid and ingenious than ever again—were undervalued. For nine months or more a year during nineteen to twenty years our occupation was learning—learning centered in a classroom—at a particular place and time, with a resource person called a teacher. Is it any wonder that we believe instinctively that education requires these things? A few fortunate ones among us were never trapped. But those of us who were (I include myself) require something close to a conversion to escape to the freedom and satisfaction of knowing that education can occur in many settings often with no classroom, no educational institution, no teacher, no formal curriculum or course plan.

THE BASIC COMPONENTS

The great variety of episodes which, when purposefully linked, form our own continuing education may be clustered in five groups. The first four comprise the educational events themselves; the fifth, those episodes in which we put the other four together.

At any given time your continuing education may involve episodes of one type or several in combination. In chapters 4 and 5 we shall look at these categories in more depth. Here we shall sketch in the basic lines of the picture as a way of further defining continuing education before we proceed.

1) *Individual study and reflection.* No matter how significant the other components, this is the foundation. Days may be missed, but continuing education which leads to competence builds study and reflection into the daily pattern of work. A primary task is to plan study efficiently in the midst of daily job and family pressures and of the knowledge explosion.

2) *Local groups.* A wide variety of group learning events can occur either at or close to our places of work. They require no break in regular routine. They range from congregational consultation-training events to study groups with professional col-

leagues or with laity to the more intentional colleague support-development groups discussed in chapter 7. Ironically, we often overlook them because they are obvious and accessible, yet they afford, along with personal study and reflection, the primary setting for continuing education.

3) *Short-term organized courses and seminars.* In the 1960s and early 1970s these have been the main fare of continuing education. When we have thought "continuing education" these programs have flashed in our minds, primarily because much of the literature has conditioned us to think that way, and, indeed, many short-term programs have been and are highly useful. Usually they last three to ten days, although I would include here those few which last a month to six weeks. For the most part they are held at a seminary, retreat center, or another agency requiring residence away from home. They most often focus on one subject or area, though some offer a smorgasbord.

I include in this category courses in seminaries, universities, community colleges, municipal adult education programs, and the like in or near one's home community, involving one or more hours a week for a semester or year and requiring no change of residence.

4) *Long-term programs.* Increasingly professionals in all fields are taking longer study leaves and sabbaticals. I use "sabbatical" for a year's leave which usually requires finding or being appointed to another job upon return. "Long-term study leave" denotes a leave of three to nine months (usually not longer than six). In many cases now local judicatories provide a temporary replacement so that a job change is not required. (I will use "sabbatical" and "long-term study leave" from here on in the same sense.)

Periods lasting three or four months can be profitable. (The Merrill Fellows program at Harvard, e.g., requires only three months away from home.) I also include in this category advanced professional degree programs. Some professionals are enrolled in Ph.D. programs, chipping away at them as they can, realizing that a time may come when a period away from the job will be required to complete them. Interest, however, is shifting rapidly to the new doctor of ministry degrees, organized with the professional especially in mind, with heavy in-service components and a minimum amount of in-residence work.

5) *Planning.* Continuing education as I have defined it requires planning. For its various episodes to be linked together in an unfolding process there must also be those episodes—short and long, formal and informal—when we plan the process. It will not happen by itself.

A major weakness in our continuing education has been that we have seen it as occasional, random participation in an educational episode. We read a book, enroll in a course, attend a seminar, and then say that we have done continuing education.

> I stick in a thumb
> And pull out a plum
> And say, "What a good boy am I."

As I have said, these individual episodes may be continuing education in a minimal sense, but only that. Effective, competence-producing continuing education will join them together in a well-thought-out plan. So important is planning that I have devoted chapters 4 and 5 to it. Together they form the heart of the book.

In one sense, planning could be seen as preparatory to continuing education. I see it, however, as integral to the process itself. Effective planning requires that you find out where you are in your career; the degree of your effectiveness; what your career goals really are; the program and other resources which can meet your needs. This in itself is an educative process. As time goes on and continuing education becomes increasingly an unfolding process, the planning episodes will be so integral to it that you will recognize them fully as part and parcel of your continuing education.

Chapter II

LIFELONG LEARNING

They had been backdoor neighbors for a year. He had often borrowed Ed's tools and welcomed his advice about fixing things around the house. Sometimes they had walked to the church together for administrative board meetings, and during these walks, as at other times, he had come to value his neighbor's gentle counsel. But last night the quality of Ed's life had struck him with a new force. The board was apparently at a dead end in its plan for a new part-time pastor's assistant. There were just too many different opinions. During a lull Ed spoke in his usual quiet way. The words were exactly right. Their good sense and the spirit of his offering combined as the catalyst that let them adjourn, not with the problem solved but with clear alternatives in view. In bed that night he had realized what a remarkable man this was. What forces and events made him what he was? What was the source of his strong but gentle spirit? What were the ingredients of his common sense? What constituted his faith? What bearing did it have on the rest of his life? These questions tumbled over one another until he finally slept.

The next few weeks were a peak learning period as he talked with Ed about his life. He knew now that the life of a fellow human being is an invaluable resource for learning.

It would be difficult to imagine a more significant learning event. Some would call it continuing education, and, I suppose, in the broadest sense it is. But I have come to think of this and informal episodes like it as parts of lifelong learning, which I distinguish from continuing education. Continuing education, as I have said, is a planned learning process with episodes that are more or less formal and organized. Lifelong learning is a highly informal process—more, in fact, an open attitude toward life.

This may seem like an artificial distinction. But if you will reserve that judgment until you have finished this chapter, perhaps you will see why I make it. For me, at least, the distinction helps clarify the meaning of continuing education and defines an attitude toward life which provides a necessary and fertile matrix for more formal and organized learning experiences.

First, let me define "lifelong learning" and then tell you how it came to be significant for me. In doing so I will be unabashedly autobiographical: *Lifelong learning is that quality of life characterized by openness to oneself, to others, and to the world, which lets learning occur anytime, anywhere, using whatever data may be available and appropriate.*

Eight years ago when I began my present job, continuing education for ministry was a movement in its exuberant childhood. I and many others saw it essentially in terms of educational programs—seminars, institutes, courses, degree programs, and the like. Soon, however, the definition stated earlier began to form (for this I owe a substantial debt to Dr. Connolly Gamble). I realized that continuing education is an unfolding process, grounded in each individual's unfolding life and work. These, not some agency's programs, are the keys to its continuities and its development.

Yet, I also realized that if continuing education were seen in this way, it would involve much more than formal and organized educational episodes. How about all the learning which goes on informally? What about the learning one gets from looking at a star? What about the discoveries when two lives meet?

It was impossible to deny that these informal and unplanned events were learning—learning often more important than that in organized events. But I had difficulty in thinking of them as continuing education without hopelessly confusing both—at least with my compulsively ordered mind.

In the mid-1960s I began to see references to "lifelong learning" in the jargon of adult education. Sometimes it was a synonym of continuing education, but more often it had its own distinct meaning. The United Nations designated 1970 as the International Education Year, and lifelong learning was mentioned frequently in the literature. Paul Lengrand described it as a "way of life and of being aware of the world." Rene Maheu said that it "represents an attitude and dimension of life." [1]

These definitions intrigued me. Neither referred to lifelong learning as a *process,* but rather as a *way* of life, an *attitude,* a *dimension.* In this, I suppose, it is like love or integrity. Both are, of course, processes; they must be acted out. But we sense their meaning most fully when we think of them as dimensions or qualities of life. Lifelong learning, it occurred to me, is also a process, but its meaning, like theirs, is most fully sensed when understood as a way or quality of life. I had arrived at the definition stated above.

THE RESOURCES FOR LIFELONG LEARNING

A major milestone in this pilgrimage was a lecture by Ivan Illych, the controversial educational theorist, one of those events which one comes upon quite by surprise. I had not planned to hear him that night, but went because some friends were going. It was a memorable evening.

Illych said that only three resources are needed for learning: objects, human models, and other persons with the same learning needs and interests. By objects he meant all material and non-material things on which our minds can focus: the vast number

[1] "1970 Named International Education Year," *Continuing Education for Adults,* 143 (December 31, 1969), 1, 2.

of objects in the natural world, books, musical compositions, motion pictures—who could name them all!

By human models he meant individuals who in themselves incorporate knowledge, skills, life-styles, work-patterns, from which we might profit. He told of an experiment in which teenage Puerto Ricans in New York city, with a modicum of instruction, had become productive instructors of spoken Spanish for Anglo workers in the city's West Side.

By the third resource, he meant that persons working together in groups on a common educational enterprise can be resources to one another. His assumption was that many people in our society have learning needs in common and would both enjoy and profit from working on them together.

The implications of Illych's idea are limitless. If the idea grabs you as it has me, you will soon spin out your own. Let me share a few of mine.

Consider objects: It so happened that as I wrote this, Wagner's Overture to Tannhauser was being broadcast on my FM radio-tape player (which itself is a significant object and purveyor of objects for my own learning). For some reason, it caught my ear, and I stopped writing to give it my full attention. The final development of its strong, beautiful theme amidst the continued cascading of the strings imaged, for some reason, the way in which deeply rooted humanizing processes can grow in the midst of social tumult. The experience will speak to me for a long time.

Raising roses is one of my hobbies. No flower, for me, has more simple grace and delicate beauty. Perhaps for that reason Gertrude Stein's poem has appeal: "Rose is a rose is a rose is a rose." The poem symbolizes the several layers of meaning which I see in a rose: its beauty, its instruction about the ways of nature, its exemplification of the mysteries of life's unfolding, its call for nurture.[2]

---

[2] Cf. Frederick S. Perls, *Gestalt Therapy Verbatim* (New York: Bantam Books, 1969), p. 4, for what he has learned from the poem.

Most intriguing is the idea of a human model as a resource for learning. The idea is certainly not new. "In many and various ways God spoke of old to our fathers by the prophets; but in these last days he has spoken to us by a son" (Heb. 1:1, 2*a*). Incorporation of God's word in a person—a human model —is what incarnation is all about.

"Model" as Illych used it, and as I use it here, does not denote an ideal example to be copied. Instead, a living example to be looked at carefully for what it can teach us for our own life patterns.

No book, no professor can tell us what the practice of ministry is so well as someone doing it competently and responsibly. Most of us can identify professional colleagues whom we respect and from whom we have learned informally a great deal about what the practice of ministry is at both its heart and periphery. Seminary educators are increasingly incorporating the human model in education for ministry through the use of pastors and other professionals as adjunct professors. I have been closely related to a major pilot project in career development for pastors between three and five years out of seminary. For approximately two years these young pastors were members of small cluster groups meeting every two weeks, usually, to work on their personal and professional development. One of the most significant elements in this program was the pastoral associate, a more experienced colleague whom the young pastors in a cluster group chose to meet with them during the two years. The pastoral associate became an integral part of the group, often working on his own development along with the young pastors. The young pastors rejected, by and large, the idea that he was a model in any sense, but time after time they probed the ways he functioned in ministry.[3]

[3] Edgar E. Mills, *Peer Groups and Professional Development: Evaluation Report of the Young Pastors Pilot Project* (Nashville: United Methodist Board of Higher Education and Ministry: Division of the Ordained Ministry, 1973), cf. especially chs. 4 and 5.

All about us in the world are human models, persons who incorporate a value, a skill, a quality, a commitment, which exemplifies humanity at its best. Most of them would be glad to talk with us about how they see their lives—its sources, its dynamics, how it feels, its hopes, frustrations.

The human model is not only the richest resource for life-long learning, it is also the most available! An object is available, of course, but it cannot be probed dialectically like the human model. Neither does it have the depth and complexity of a person. Yet, strangely, we use this resource so little. During my eleven years as a pastor I can identify few times when I have sat down with another person whose life I admired in some way to let him or her share with me the nature and dynamics of what they incorporated. I fear that many of us are similarly impover-ished in the midst of wealth.

Illych believes that in a "deschooled" society, individuals with similar needs and interests would find one another and join in dyads or other groups to pursue their common aim. This very linkage would itself be a resource.

I question whether the grouping would happen as naturally as he thinks (but who knows, since we do not have a deschooled society). For several years some students at the Harvard Graduate School of Education have experimented with asking persons to state learning needs, feeding these into a computer, finding the groupings which emerge, and notifying those who fall into similar groups. The project has met with modest success.

I would add another resource to Illych's three, one's own life. Your own life is the most immediate resource you possess. In one sense it is an object, but an object sufficiently unique to be in a category by itself. The human being participates uniquely in the subject-object dialectic.

Reflection on experience is the primary mode through which this resource becomes available. The experiences to be reflected upon range all the way from the most intimate and delicate perceptions of the core of one's existence to the most structured procedures involved in one's work. Life inevitably gets lived; experience comes willy-nilly. The question is, will it be reflected upon in such a way that we will learn from it? Wasn't it one of the pioneers of lifelong learning who said, The unexamined life is not worth living?

Whether or not we learn from our experience depends upon our openness to ourselves. When I stand back and look it often seems exceedingly strange that we build walls, impenetrable and opaque, which shield us from ourselves. I think I understand some of the psychological dynamics; but isn't it strange, nevertheless? In any case, to learn from ourselves the walls must come down. This is not a book focused on personal development, so I will not pursue this further except to say that as the walls do come down we have our own authentic experience available to us as a resource for lifelong learning. Once available, we must make conscious choices and develop skills in reflecting on our experiences.

Later, we will consider reflection on our work as a major resource for continuing education. But reflection on work will be impoverished and deceptive if we are unable to reflect upon ourselves.

THE NONDISCIPLINE OF LIFELONG LEARNING

We are accustomed to think that education and learning require stringent discipline. They do.

Paradoxically, lifelong learning, as I have interpreted it, requires a large portion of "nondiscipline." One reason, perhaps the major reason, that we do not learn from the world around and within is that we hold ourselves too tightly in check. To put it simply: to be open is to be relaxed. Not lazy, relaxed. The mind hell-bent on the rational pursuit of an idea may miss a momentary experience of beauty which will never reappear or an insight which the unconscious would like to offer but cannot from its prison cell.

Two dynamics inhibit the nondiscipline of lifelong learning. One is the neurotic compulsion that causes us to defend ourselves from experiences which come too close to us personally. Disciplined work (not neurotic in itself) is one of our most effective defense mechanisms.

The other dynamic is more purely cognitive—simply the notion that any learning requires disciplined control. It does of course—at certain times and in certain cases. But not always. To master the key concepts of Bonhoeffer's thought requires controlled discipline, but to sense the key dynamics of another person's life requires relaxed openness.

These barriers must come down if we are to experience fully the quality of life that I have referred to here as lifelong learning. To appropriate the resources that surround us we must walk through the world with the delicate sensors of life exposed.

LIFELONG LEARNING AND CONTINUING EDUCATION

This, then, is what I mean by lifelong learning. And for me it is useful to distinguish it from continuing education. It may help clarify the distinction to place the two definitions side by side.

Lifelong learning is that quality of life characterized by openness to oneself, to others, and to the world which lets learning occur anytime, anywhere, using whatever data may be available and appropriate.

Continuing education is an individual's personally designed learning program which begins when basic formal education ends and continues throughout a career and beyond. An unfolding process, it links together personal study and reflection and participation in organized group events.

Continuing education comprises a related series of more-or-less organized events. Thought of in this way, it becomes a manageable object for analysis and planning.

But we learn in many other ways highly informal, unorganized, and often surprising. These we can think of in terms of lifelong learning, realizing that at many points in life itself the boundaries between it and continuing education become fuzzy or disappear. (Many things distinguishable on the pages of a book are inseparable in life!) Many of the surprising, momentary experiences of lifelong learning, for example, will intrude into the most carefully planned seminar.

From this point, we will focus on continuing education, but with the awareness that lifelong learning is its matrix.

Chapter III

THE CRISIS OF COMPETENCE

The primary aim of continuing education is to produce growing competence. All learning has inherent values, but continuing education is not an end in itself. In simple systems language it looks like this:

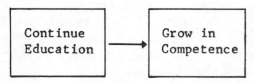

Erase the arrow or divert it, and not only is growing competence impossible, but continuing education has little point and may, in fact, be destructive.

One value in thinking of the minister or other paid church leader as a professional is that the professional's learning is for the sake of competent practice. That is, by definition, part of what it means to be a professional. The professional person engages in learning for the sake of others. He or she learns in order to be competent, in order to serve.

I know the problems in thinking of ourselves as professionals. Our society is plagued by self-serving professionalism. The remedy for that, however, is not to deny that we are professionals, but to exemplify the responsible acceptance of the role. The words of Van A. Harvey in his much discussed article of several years ago "On Separating Hopes from Illusions" are still relevant. Bishop J. A. T. Robinson had spoken in Dallas saying that the church should look forward to the day of a nonprofessional lay ministry. Harvey replied:

> If the mission of the church is to permeate and mold the institutions of the world, then it could be said that a more devastating criticism of the church is not that it is professional but that it is not professional enough; that it is ingrown, mediocre, concerned with the wrong things, unwise in its allocation of resources and naive in its conception of the problems of modern man. In short, it is amateur.
>
> There is, I believe, something primitive, something romantic, in Robinson's appeal to Paul the tentmaker as a model for the twentieth-century minister. What we need is a highly skilled, trained, intelligent, articulate professional class which is in contact with the world and its centers of power. We need a clergy that knows the world better than the world knows itself and that is able, therefore, to interpret this world so that Christians may be at home in it, act in it, love it, and take responsibility for it. And it is just because we do not have such a conception of the clergy that it is increasingly being regarded by the most thoughtful and idealistic young people as a vocation unworthy of their aspirations and abilities. They believe it is neither a demanding nor an influential means of service in the modern world.[1]

I would not do battle for a term. If clinging to "professional" will prevent our acting effectively and responsibly in our vocation we should abandon it. But I feel relatively sure that if we said—all of us—tomorrow that we are not professionals, the abuses would still be there. When, on the other hand, we understand the long and respectable history of the professions in our culture, the term can remind us that practice uninformed by the right kind of learning is irresponsible and that the pur-

---

[1] *motive*, November 1965, pp. 4-5. While agreeing heartily with the main thrust of this statement, I would disagree with its apparent implication that no legitimate place exists for a tentmaking ministry.

pose of learning is to help produce the competence that will make possible a servant profession.[2]

By competence, I mean the ability to do well the job required of us, recognizing that differing clusters of competencies are required in different types of professional leadership. Dr. Henry Adams has pointed out a helpful distinction between competence and effectiveness. "It is important," he says, "to distinguish competence from effectiveness. . . . Education alone, in the conventional sense, is no guarantee of effectiveness." For example, "A clergyman who wants people to be engaged in social action as an expression of their faith may be competent in the social implications of the religious heritage. But without laymen who understand and trust his leadership, he may be a lonely and ineffectual person."[3]

As I discuss competence, this is a useful distinction to keep in mind. Competence will not necessarily produce effectiveness, and effectiveness is our aim. From competence to effectiveness, however, is a short step when competence is broad enough to include the knowledge and skill that effectiveness requires. So here our focus is on competence, but always with the awareness that, like continuing education, it is not an end in itself. The design would look like this:

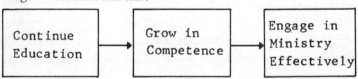

---

[2] There is a growing body of literature on the nature of a profession and the ministry as a profession. James D. Glasse in *Profession: Minister* (Nashville: Abingdon Press, 1968) called to our attention again the usefulness of the term, though it has weaknesses which some of its reviews have pointed out. Urban I. Holmes III's more recent book *The Future Shape of Ministry* (New York: The Seabury Press, 1971) contains several useful chapters on the ministry as a profession (cf. especially chs. 10 and 13). A useful analysis is: Everett C. Hughes, "The Professions in Society," *Canadian Journal of Economics and Political Science,* 26 February 1964), 54-61.

[3] "Effectiveness in Ministry: A Proposal for Lay-Clergy Collegiality," *The Christian Ministry,* January 1973, p. 32.

THE CRISIS OF COMPETENCE

As a profession, we are in a crisis of competence. Our growth in effectiveness is not keeping pace with what the church and the world, implicitly and explicitly, are asking of us. Not only do we recognize the crisis in our profession generally, but many of us experience it personally. We know that we ourselves are in a crisis of competence.

For example, we met the death of God theology with a "great volley of shudders." [4] We, with our people, had said, "I believe in God the Father almighty"—or something like it— each Sunday for years. Yet when a small group of theologians, each in his own way, said God had died, and "theology by journalism" spread the word, thousands of us responded with silence, shudders, or raving. We could not say how persons in a secular, twentieth-century culture can indeed believe in God. A decade later, we are still unsure.[5] This is partially a crisis of the spirit. In no small measure, however, it is a crisis of competence.

A mother comes to her minister of education bewildered by the sex ethic of her teen-age daughter. She senses that it is a genuine ethic, however different from hers. Her daughter is far less promiscuous, she believes, than many of her own middle-age friends. But she wants to know how to understand her daughter's ethic and how it relates to Christian ethics. They have talked only an hour, when the most sensitive problem emerges. The mother herself is ethically at sea, *but* her counselor is also at sea: (1) The counselor comprehends not at all the ethic by which the girl is working out her life; (2) The counselor's understanding of Christian ethics is a combination of nine-

[4] Borden Parker Bowne's description of the response of the American clergy of his generation to the threatening philosophy of Herbert Spencer.

[5] Generalizations are always risky. There are, of course, many highly positive, encouraging exceptions to the generalizations in this section and the following one.

teenth-century moralism and the Ten Commandments, mixed with a smattering of grace. She has known for five years that she should probe the real meaning of Christian ethics—but how to find time. She suddenly feels the exposed raw nerve of her incompetence.

Conflict breaks out in the congregation. Having smoldered for months, it finally erupts. The pastor knows that there are proven techniques for enabling groups to deal with conflict, but he has learned none of them. He wonders whether he has procrastinated because to learn the techniques would force a look at himself which he dreads. Before he acts the conflict becomes destructive.

As a profession and as individuals we are in a crisis of competence. Our vocational health as individuals, but more important the health of the church, is bound up in this crisis. Since competence and continuing education are vitally linked, examination of the crisis should shed light on the basic concern of this book.

Jeffrey K. Hadden in *The Gathering Storm in the Churches* identified four crises in the American church—three faced by professional leaders and laity together, one by professional leaders alone.[6] The crisis of competence is so interlaced with these that a brief reminder of their character will be useful:

1) The crisis of meaning and purpose. Is the church's pur-

---

[6] (New York: Doubleday & Co., 1969), pp. 3-33, 212-21. Data gathered prior to 1969 runs the risk of being obsolete. Hadden in a more recent article, "The Gathering Storm Revisited," *Journal* (United Church of Christ), 1 (Spring 1972), claims that the crises are still present. His opening comment bears quoting: "For a number of years, scholars have been telling religious leaders that the institutional church is in deep trouble. Today a fairly large proportion seem to have accepted some version of this interpretation of reality. Yet, to an outside observer, the response of church leaders to this crisis is hard to comprehend. There remains an Alice-in-Wonderland, business-as-usual quality to their life styles. Perhaps this is because only a very few have grasped the full implications of the storm which lies ahead."

pose to provide comfort and repose or to *"challenge* men to put an end to social injustice in the world"?

2) The crisis of belief. "Theologies which a few years ago would have been thought of as heresy are now being received with interest and even enthusiasm in some circles. Among clergy and laity there is a great deal of doubt and division of opinion as to what constitutes appropriate belief." One might add that this crisis has been given a new dimension and added urgency through the various current manifestations of the Spirit Movement.

3) The crisis of authority. "In Protestantism today, laity, who have entrusted authority to professional leaders, have come to have grave doubts about how the authority has been used, and are beginning to assert their own influence." The crisis of authority in Roman Catholicism is no less severe.

4) The professional leader's own crisis of identity. In part, it results from the other three. It has also its own sources. Our role, says Hadden, is today highly ambiguous. Society no longer assigns it to us clearly, and we seem unable to shape it ourselves. More crucial is our role in relation to the community's values. "But what happens when a human community's values are in a state of flux or transition? To be sure, if the changing values are central to every individual, the entire community experiences some strain. But the strain is most acute for those whose responsibility it is to define, sustain, and transmit the values in question. When the values in flux are as basic as the ultimate meaning of life itself, the amount of strain is understandably great." [7]

To these I would add the crisis of competence. What are its sources? Many, but I will focus on three.

1) Our neglect of the more-or-less standard competencies which our profession requires, and will continue to require, as well as the particular ones germane to its various particular jobs.

2) A failure of nerve caused, to a great extent, by the four

[7] *The Gathering Storm,* pp. 6, 26 30, 212.

crises that Hadden has identified. The crisis of competence is in this sense a function of the other four. To renew and sustain growing competence is an arduous responsibility. When the nerve to our psychic energies is cut, we simply do not get at it; it becomes well-nigh impossible.

3) Change. I suspect that most of us are up to our ears in talk about change. Furthermore, we read and discuss a book like *Future Shock* and its exciting predictions, without really thinking through its implications for our profession.[8] My suspicion grows that playing games with futurism (itself a valid pursuit) is a way of shielding ourselves from the real, present effects of change—now.

So much has been written and spoken about societal change as a reason for continuing education that to say much more easily becomes a play in the futurism game. So one statement is enough. It goes so incisively to the heart of the matter that it is the one symbol which I personally have needed these past eight years (although I too find my head spinning and my heart palpitating when I hear of new manifestations of these words). Dr. Huston Smith of MIT at the first major consultation on continuing education for ministry said:

From the millions of words that have been written about change in our time—its acceleration and its crescendo—two phrases endure. The first is by Whitehead, who saw the modern world as issuing from "the invention of invention." More far-reaching than any specific discovery in the scientific revolution was the discovery of a technique for building discovery itself into the fabric of Western civilization. The consequences of this metadiscovery are gathered in the second phrase, by Robert Oppenheimer: "the prevalence of newness." The thing that is new, he wrote in 1955, "is newness, the changing scale and scope of change itself, so that the world alters as we walk on it, so that the years of a man's life measure not some

[8] Alvin Toffler (New York: Random House, 1970).

37

small growth or rearrangement or moderation of what he learned in childhood but a great upheaval.[9]

Two aspects of this great upheaval most strikingly affect our professional competence. First, changes in society that make increasingly complex the application of the gospel. If Judaeo-Christian faith tended toward withdrawal from the world, societal change would be interesting but not crucially important. Exactly the opposite is true. Our faith thrusts us out into the world as its interpreters (as Van Harvey said, it is our business "to know the world better than the world knows itself") and with the message of liberation and reconciliation. If we have not the slightest idea of what is happening to the world—really, how can we possibly interpret it to itself and help achieve liberation and reconciliation?

Secondly, the radical change affects the way all of us experience existence in the world. This is not the first time that our race has experienced a radical revision of its world view. But that fact is no help. *It is happening now.* As before in history, the faith needs to be retranslated to make it comprehensible for contemporary experience.[10] That is too important a task for the theologians—alone. They, church professional leaders and the laity, must be about it together. No task imaginable has closer interrelationships with the crisis of competence.

THE DRIVE FOR COMPETENCE

Another major dimension of the crisis which is exceedingly hopeful is the human drive for competence. A true crisis is never made up of only negative forces. It is always a clash between opposing forces: $+ \longleftrightarrow -$. The negative force in this case is

[9] "Education in a Changing World," *Proceedings of the Consultation on Continuing Education,* Ralph E. Peterson, ed. (New York: National Council of Churches of Christ in the U.S.A., Department of Ministry, 1968), p. 9.

[10] For an insightful analysis of the way we experience the world today and its implications for faith, I would recommend Langdon Brown Gilkey, *Naming the Whirlwind* (Indianapolis: Bobbs-Merrill, 1969), cf. especially Part I, "The Challenge to God Language."

our lack of competence. The drive for competence is a strong positive force. A resolution of the crisis not only starts moving us toward competence, it also releases our drive for that quality.

Deep within our nature lodges a strong drive for competence. When released or activated, it can be a strong motivating force for doing those things—including continued education—which make for competence. It can also produce a highly pleasurable but solid sense of satisfaction and well-being. It bears examination.

Think about your childhood. It is remarkable how much of your early growth and development was a matter of acquiring competence. You learned *how to* say hundreds of words and what they meant. You learned *how to* interpret, as a baby, the looks on your mother's face, even the feel of her hands. You learned *how to* pick up and shake a rattle to give pleasure, and gradually you acquired skill in using hundreds of tools. You learned *how to* think, first about concrete objects and then about intangible ideas.

Jean Piaget, still actively working at the Jean-Jacques Rousseau Institute in Geneva, has built one of the most intriguing and influential educational theories of our time. Based on observation of thousands of children, including his own, the theory is that growth in the ability to think (cognition) is a process of being able to carry out, first, "concrete operations" (using material objects) and then "formal operations" (using ideas independently of material objects).[11] Actually, Piaget is saying that from birth through adolescence (where his study ends) growth is a matter of gradually increasing competence— acquiring "means sufficient for the necessities of life."[12]

The drive for competence as a central and determinative factor in personality formation has been explicitly developed by

[11] For a succinct discussion of Piaget and his thought, cf. Herbert Ginsburg and Sylvia Opper, *Piaget's Theory of Intellectual Development: An Introduction* (Englewood Cliffs, N.J.: Prentice-Hall, 1969).

[12] *Webster's Seventh New Collegiate Dictionary*, s.v. "competence."

Robert W. White. White observed systematically the lives of fifty adults during a ten-year period. He found that competence, especially competence in human interaction, was a key to understanding their development. Lacking competence, their development was seriously impeded; with it, development was healthy.[13]

Just to be a human being is to have an astounding record (unless something was dreadfully wrong) of growing competence. One primary way to describe a human being, in fact, is as a highly competent animal—light years ahead of any other. We live through few days without saying to ourselves, "I wish I were more competent." What we may not realize is that the wish is only the tip of an iceberg—an iceberg made of fire.

Activating the drive for competence is not difficult, unless it has been seriously repressed. The chances are high that it is actively at work, in which case the first step is to recognize what is happening. For example, the drive may be highly motivating you to learn how to sail or garden or play tennis. Identifying it in such activities will give you a hint of its power. The next step will be to choose a limited new competence which you want—in this case stay away from *ought to* and stick to *want*— to have in your work. A better understanding of a key chapter from one of the Gospels, more skill in hospital calling, inside knowledge of a major business employing your lay persons. There are a hundred options. Just be sure it is attainable and go after it. Then watch what happens to you when you have it. Your self-esteem will be higher; your self-confidence will move up a notch. But the primary result will be a desire for more competence. Each new level will further unleash the drive. You will have found a major motivating force for your continuing education.

[13] Robert W. White, *Lives in Progress: A Study of the Natural Growth of Personality* (New York: Holt, Rinehart and Winston, 1952). Cf. also "Competence and Socialization" by M. Brewster Smith, in *Socialization and Society,* John A. Clausen, ed. (Boston: Little Brown, 1968), pp. 270 ff.

WHO IS THE COMPETENT PROFESSIONAL IN MINISTRY?

To describe the competent professional today is a bit more difficult than for Isaac Walton to describe *The Compleat Angler.* To catalog incompetencies is much simpler.

Professional expressions of ministry are highly varied. The competence required of the hospital chaplain is different from that of a community organizer. The pastor in Cherokee, Kansas, must have competencies not required of the prison chaplain at Leavenworth. And so it goes.

Competence is partially the expression of life-style, and a wide variety is authentic for engagement in ministry professionally. Several years ago a friend pointed out that Hawkeye in the movie M.A.S.H. is one authentic model of professional life today: a high degree of skill operative in an absurd world; immediate response to critical need; the ability to scoff at all pretentiousness. I agree. Yet, for another kind of person to try to put it together that way would be phony. Life-styles do vary, and professional styles vary with them.

The competencies required of our profession are now being summarized in statements from clergy associations, seminaries, and various other groups. To adopt any of them uncritically would be to mistake their intent. They do serve, however, as a useful starting point for an individual alone or preferably with a congregation or colleague group to formulate the competence required of that person in a given setting. A statement receiving widening attention has been compiled by a task force of the Academy of Parish Clergy (cf. Appendix I). Fully as important as the particular competencies it lists is its being a product of our profession's taking responsibility for itself, in this case, defining its own competence. Two seminaries which, in consultation with professionals and laity, have produced statements of competency are Boston University School of Theology and Union Theological Seminary, Richmond. There are probably others.

Competent Ministry

One especially useful statement was the product of a consultation on continuing education called by The United Methodist Church in 1968, which included a large proportion of pastors and other local church professional leaders.[14]

1) Professional knowledge, skills, and perspectives necessary to carry out one's work
   —Development and strengthening of special skills according to one's specific calling
   —Correcting weaknesses where a specific job requires it
   —Knowledge of and ability to use a method of evaluating one's effectiveness, including accountability to institutional supervisors

2) Perspectives upon the local congregation or other group with which the professional shares ministry
   —Theological understanding of the mission of the church
   —Ability to use the social sciences to illumine the dynamics of congregational life
   —Experience in the effective introduction of change and the constructive use of conflict

3) Self-examination and personal growth, insofar as these are necessary to professional effectiveness. (This assumes that who and what one is as a person influences effectiveness more than in some other professions.)
   —Unifying a self-image in the midst of widely diverse roles and demands
   —Inclusion of some continuing education opportunities for the professional's spouse
   —Knowledge of and willingness to utilize group and individual therapy resources when appropriate

[14] *Proceedings, Consultation on Continuing Education for Ministry*, pp. 110-12. Because the statement was formulated as a definition of the needs of the minister in continuing education, it has been editorially restated at points for use here.

4) Data and theoretical perspectives to understand the changing world in which the minister works
   —A method of theological reflection
   —Knowledge of and experience in using psychological and social processes to minister to persons, structures, and issues

5) Identity and effectiveness as a person of Christian faith able to communicate a living tradition to the world

As we discuss the planning of our own programs of continuing education in the next chapter, I will make reference to the use of this and other statements.

The competencies listed in these statements can be summarized in three basic categories. I would add a fourth, imagination.

1) *The ability to function freely and fully as a person.* That, in turn, has several major ingredients. One is a sense of self-identity, including that mysterious awareness that I am who I am, as well as knowledge of strengths and weaknesses—both those which can be modified and those which cannot. Another is freedom to function as one decides to function, granted that the decision is responsible. Another is the ability to establish and maintain open, warm, caring relationships.

The motto of my alma mater is, "Let him first be a man" (the college may one day soon have to footnote the last word). Even so, it is a good motto which means considerably more to me now than it did as a collegian. I believe (and this is one of my strongest personal convictions) that only to the degree that we achieve personhood can we achieve authentic proficiency or competence in any particular function of life. Thus, I place competence as a person first among those required for ministry. It is the soil in which all other competency grows. Carlyle Marney has said that "I am" is the basic verb of human existence. Until one can say that with certainty, he can say little else authentically.[15]

[15] "Interpreter's House: A Way Station for Understanding," *Thesis Theological Cassettes,* Vol. 3, No. 2.

2) *Knowledge.* That is the plainest word I know for this competency. By it I mean, first, knowing relevant facts. Somehow in this day that statement seems hopelessly antiquated. Nevertheless, it is true. To know, for example, as precisely as possible the significant events and cultural conditions which prevailed in the Near East in the first half of the first century affects markedly one's ability to interpret and understand the Christ-event. Knowledge also connotes a memory bank of ideas and combinations of ideas. In relation to Christian doctrine, in relation to the nature of persons, in relation to society and culture, in relation to many things, ideas are our stock-in-trade. We dare not think that, like a goose, we can wake up in a new world each morning and accumulate the ideas needed for that day. We need growing superstructures of combined ideas with which to relate new ideas and facts which we encounter.

The more pluralistic our society becomes and the more rapidly and radically our culture changes, the more we need to know about our Judaeo-Christian tradition. The crisis of faith is not just a crisis of the spirit, it is also a crisis of the mind. Many of us have simply forgotten how we got here from our slavery in Egypt.

Furthermore, now as always the Christian tradition is subject to distortion. Curiously, the closer that distortion is to the truth the more destructive it may become. Marcion's heresy was so dangerous, not because it wildly differed from the tradition, but because in many ways it was so deceptively close. Right now, the dangers of a national religion in the United States spring partially from the nearness of our national heresy to the truth. To know our tradition well—without dogmatism and with an understanding of its aliveness—has never been more important. That requires knowledge.

But mastery of our tradition is more than knowing what has happened. The tradition is to a great extent the interpretation of what has happened, and since tradition is "the living faith of dead men" (in contrast to traditionalism, which is "the dead faith of living men"),[16] it is subject to constant reinterpretation. Reinterpretations spill over one another so rapidly these days that many of us find ourselves bewildered. We barely grasp one theology when another is acclaimed as superseding it. The learning task in this bewildering milieu is to grasp as best we can the significant reinterpretations which appear, but more important, to find an open, flexible understanding to which we can commit ourselves.

3) *Skills.* A professional by definition engages in a practice which meets a major social need. A practice requires skills. Each profession has its own set (some are cross-professional). No one leaves seminary with sufficient skill for the remainder of a career. In fact, the best time seriously to approach skill development is soon after full-time professional practice has begun, and the requirements of the job are experienced daily. But more of that later.

No skill is more crucial than the ability to effect change—both within the congregation and within society. Social change skills include goal-setting, conflict-resolution, and the like; they also include knowledge of how social structures function, especially in the use of power, and those vulnerable points at which intervention makes a difference. This latter requires direct contact and often involvement with the structures. The social change skills of the professional must include the ability to train others in their use; the leader-enabler role is impossible without it.[17]

4) *Imagination.* Deliver me from the knowledgeable, skillful professional with no imagination! Imagination is a delicate quality hard to define, mysterious in its source, but without which we are heavy-handed and boring. With it we are able to venture

[16] A statement of Jarislov Pelikan quoted by Martin Marty in *Context*, August 1 and 15, 1972.
[17] The Reverend Richard Murray, Director of Continuing Education, Perkins School of Theology, has summarized the competencies required for ministry as: 1) capacity for—; 2) skills in—; 3) knowledge of—; 4) involvement with—; unpublished paper, 1972.

beyond where we are; with it we can be debonair; with it we can fantasize new ways for ministry to find expression; with it we can put our ideas together in new combinations.

Imagination is a power which we all possess innately. We do not have to import it as we do ideas and facts. Transactional Analysis theory says that our "child" ego state contains what some call the "little professor."

> The Little Professor is that part of the Child ego state that is innately
>   intuitive,
>   creative,
>   manipulative.
> With no knowledge of psychology, a child intuits much of what is going on. He looks at his mother's face and figures out he'd better stop what he's doing. He catches her nonverbal message sent through a disapproving look and responds to it. He then attempts to solve his problem with the use of his Little Professor who "psychs out" the best move in a given situation. . . .
>
> People who express their creativity purposefully use their Little Professor in conjunction with their Adult ego state. When a person experiences a moment of genius, his Little Professor is probably in on it. The Adult and the Little Professor make a good team.[18]

Especially, we might add, when it comes to professional competence.

Competence, like maturity, is dynamic and developmental. It either grows or deteriorates. We do not achieve competence, package it and possess it for the rest of our lives. Therefore I

[18] Muriel James and Dorothy Jongeward, *Born to Win: Transactional Analysis with Gestalt Experiments* (Reading, Mass.: Addison-Wesley Publishing Co., 1971), pp. 125, 126. For a unique approach to the way in which imagination can be released in the creative process, cf. George Prince, *The Practice of Creativity* (New York: Harper & Row, 1970).

reaffirm that throughout this book when I speak of competence I mean a continuing process of growth. We achieve a level of competence and then build toward the next. There are, of course, plateaus; growth in competence has a rhythm of achievement and rest as does maturing.

Chapter IV

PUTTING IT ALL TOGETHER: A GUIDE TO PLANNING

Before he sets out, the traveller must possess fixed interests and faculties, to be served by travel. If he drifted aimlessly from country to country he would not *travel* but only wander, ramble or tramp. The traveller must be somebody and come from somewhere, so that his definite character and moral traditions may supply an origin and a point of comparison for his observations. He must not go nosing about like a peddler for profit or like an emigrant for a vacant lot. Everywhere he should show the discretion and maintain the dignity of a guest. Everywhere he should remain a stranger no matter how benevolent, and a critic no matter how appreciative. Were he a mere sensorium, without his own purposes, moral categories and points of reference, he might as well have left those variegated natives to lead their lives undisturbed and unvisited. They would have gone on the more comfortably without him, and he the more inexpensively without them, at home. The traveller should be an artist recomposing what he sees; then he can carry away the picture and add it to a transmissible fund of wisdom, not as further miscellaneous experience but as a corrected view of the truth.[1]

Too often continuing education is aimless drifting. Any real traveler will wander on occasion, but that is different. We are travelers, not wanderers. The primary aim of this chapter is to enhance the journey.

[1] George Santayana.

Putting It All Together: A Guide to Planning

Continuing education, as I define it, is an individual's own sustained and unfolding program of education—a more prosaic way of saying that it is a journey.

Dr. Connolly C. Gamble, Jr. said in 1966, "Such education . . . involves a *system* or program. It must have a plan. It does not just 'happen'—it requires deliberate conception. It seeks for an order that will make study consecutive and cumulative. It adopts a purpose, sifts through many possibilities, and retains those pursuits that promise to advance that purpose." [2]

This means of course that you are the one primarily responsible for planning. In this sense you are the dean of your own continuing education. This book in its entirety is designed to help you invent a plan and carry it out; this chapter and the next, however, are written with that especially in view.

Before proceeding, let's look briefly again at the implication of your assuming primary responsibility for your own plan. Why your own plan? Why your own responsibility? Why can't a seminary or some other agency plan it for you? *Because you yourself are the clue to its objectives and organization. Your* work, *your* life, in their unfolding development are its primary determinants. No school, no organization can second guess how your needs and interests will develop. They can estimate that there are general needs which are widely felt and plan programs accordingly. But the basic curriculum or plan for your continuing education is your own, and you alone must take responsibility for it. "An adult learner's commitments are acknowledged to be, first to his own business and desires. The field of his own choice. . . . The learning of *his* lesson is *his* triumph, not the teacher's." [3]

This may seem too heavy. I can hear some of you say: "He must be kidding. I've managed to attend some continuing educa-

[2] "The Continuing Education of the Minister," *Proceedings, 1966 Navy Supervistory Chaplains Conference* (Washington, D.C.: Bureau of Naval Personnel: Chaplains Division, 1966), p. 226.
[3] Horace M. Kallen, *The Continuing Task* (Center for Study of Liberal Education for Adults [CSLEA] pamphlet #54), p. 26.

tion programs and just barely keep up on my reading. Now he says I have to plan a curriculum of study. Forget it!"

I can understand this reaction. Time is a scarce resource. We all face many days when the thought of one more heavy responsibility is intolerable. However, time for planning can well be a replacement, not an addition. Far better to eliminate a continuing education program or a book and work at mapping out the journey than to continue aimless wandering.

More important, when you get the taste of creative planning with a colleague group, through a career evaluation, with an expert counselor, you will find it satisfying. And the satisfaction will grow as you experience growing competence because of well-planned continuing education.

The plan for your continuing education will likely not be elaborate. If you like elaborate plans, more power to you, but an effective plan can be quite simple, especially in its beginning. Several years ago a friend of mine read Elizabeth O'Connor's *Journey Inward, Journey Outward,*[4] in which she describes the effect which a study of the Psalms had on the personal life and ministry of Gordon Cosby, pastor of the Church of the Saviour (about which the book was written). My friend was intrigued and laid out a simple plan for a several months study of the Psalms. He was thus underway with a simple but effective plan. That, I would hope, was not the end of his planning, but it was a beginning.

A plan for continuing education is goal-oriented. A traveler is going somewhere. Side trips along the way are fun, but a series of destinations are always in view—destinations, by the way, which sometimes change as travel proceeds.

The plan is, at the same time, flexible. Goals change as life and work change. Also, a plan is unfolding; one thing, when exciting, often leads to another (see sample plan, pp. 63-64).

[4] (New York: Harper & Row, 1968).

As a guide for planning, I will suggest, first, a brief case study; then several basic questions which will be continually recycled in planning; finally, the basic steps. At the chapter's close I will comment briefly on two special matters: the study leave and the professional doctorate.

A CASE STUDY

Suppose we go back to the beginning of chapter 1 and pick up the case of the pastor whose congregation is engaged in a consultation (his name, by the way, will be Elliot). New life and hope emerged in the congregation during the consultation. But one important side benefit resulted from the discussion of Elliot's preaching. He acknowledged that night what he had known for months but hadn't admitted to himself: he was capable of far better preaching. To improve his preaching had become a new career goal within a few weeks.

It was Elliot's turn to present a case study to his monthly colleague group meeting. He decided to write up the process that had led to the new goal and ask the group to help him clarify it and find resources for working toward it. From the discussion three conclusions emerged: 1) work on exegesis and the analysis of contemporary society were more needed than training in communication skills; 2) a nearby seminary had a skilled professor in biblical exegesis. During the third quarter Elliot could take a three-hour course with no major break in parish responsibilities; 3) several group members expressed a need for a fresh look at contemporary society. They decided that another colleague, Bob, would bring a preliminary study design to the next session and that they would make their meetings biweekly in order to have twelve sessions for the study before summer. They agreed also that Elliot would occasionally test his learnings from the exegesis study in relation to their study of society.

But what about the congregation's new provision of study leave time? Elliot agreed with the new congregational committee that the time for the course would be equivalent to the leave for this year. The grant would go toward tuition.

Another idea gradually took shape for the following year. His fortieth birthday had been unexpectedly difficult. Elliot had often remembered jokingly his father's dread of the decade birthdays. But this year, it was less a joke. Several things had happened recently that seemed in some vague way related to this birthday. He'd just barely missed becoming the pastor of St. John's. No great blow, but he'd wanted it. Years ago he had often wondered if he really should be a minister, but that question had been settled—so he thought. But in the days of tension before the consultation, the old question was back.

Why not get an assessment at a career development center in place of a more usual continuing education program? He decided to. It turned out to be one of his most productive decisions. From the tests, the interviews, his own reflection during the three days and two follow-up visits, several results stood out: 1) He better understood the reasons for uneasiness about turning forty and had put in perspective some other feelings and questions related to the entrance into mid-career; 2) there were unexpected results from further exploration of his skill development in preaching. His colleagues had been right about his communication skills. They were based, he found, in native ability. His study of exegesis and contemporary society had been productive, but had left a nagging sense of something unfinished which he couldn't identify. As he talked with the career counselor, he gradually realized what it was. He was not all that sure inwardly of the faith he had been proclaiming. Almost immediately he perceived a relationship between that and the sense that he was never completely "present" when he preached the sermon itself. He wasn't sure what he would do with his discovery; deep personal issues were involved. But, at least, he now knew the core issue, and he found satisfaction in that. 3) The tests produced a quite unexpected result. On the one hand, he had expressed "people concerns" as a high value; on the other, he had registered low in empathetic skills. Maybe Jim in that first conversation during the consultation had really been saying: "Elliot, I don't hear you really speaking to *me* when you preach; I'm not sure you really *understand* me. Maybe you've never really *heard* me."

A number of elements fell into place. While at the center and in the ensuing weeks Elliot put together a two-year plan for his continuing education. He knew it would likely be modified as he went along, but it was a definite plan with clear steps moving toward a newly established goal.

Thursday morning his monthly cassette tape came. He listened to it, especially to the exegesis of the parable of the friend at midnight, and mailed it on to the next member of their round-robin subscription group.

FOUR QUESTIONS

Planning involves four basic questions that have a logical sequence. Sometimes you will ask them in combination or in another order, but none can be left out. They will be continually recycled.

1) *What do I need?* The question sounds individualistic, but it is not intended to be. Perhaps it should be: What do *we* need? i.e., What does my congregation (or other employer) need from my leadership? What do I need to do to enable the church to fulfill its mission?

Even though my sense of need takes these questions fully into account, even though I plan collaboratively and recognize my accountability, the basic question comes back to my own sense of need. I must finally make the decisions; I must finally accept responsibility for what I decide.

Personal and professional growth are inseparable, and they have a unique linkage in our development as church professionals. Yet it is useful to separate them in the initial approach to the need question.

First, then: What do I need personally? What does my personal growth require? Throughout life six primary processes of growth are essential. Growth in (1) clarity and strength of personal identity; (2) in the ability to feel accurately one's primary emotions; (3) in openness to the world, especially to other persons; (4) in freedom; (5) in the ability to decide; (6) in depth of commitment to one's chosen values. Asking ourselves what personal growth requires, we can scarcely escape examination of ourselves in relation to these processes.

Personal growth often has specific bearing on growth in a professional skill. Growth in openness, e.g., is bound to affect one's preaching and teaching skills and many other aspects of professional practice. But in the long run, the more significant bearing is simply that the more fully human we are the more effectively we function in all aspects of life, including our work. Thus, the first question always is: What do I, at this point, need to do in order to grow as a human being?

The other question, or the other part of the same question is: What do I need in order to grow professionally? Asking that may force us back to personal growth questions. When Elliot asked more about his preaching skill during the career assessment, he was forced back to two very personal issues: his faith commitment and his openness to others. It may also force us back to basic questions about ministry. That many of us today are unsure of the nature of ministry—ordained or lay—goes almost without saying. To ask the question seriously may seem troublesome, but it may be one of the most crucial in the whole process.

Beyond these foundational questions are many particular ones: Where am I in my career? What skills do I need? What new knowledge do I need? What knowledge needs updating or reintegrating with my work responsibilities?

One word of caution: be careful to distinguish *wants* and *needs*. Sometimes they are the same, but sometimes we are deceived. I may *want* to study theology when I *need* to learn to communicate. I may *want* to attend another human relations lab when I *need* to acquaint myself with that part of the changing city that surrounds my church building. Assistance in making this distinction is a major benefit of consultation in planning. To see ourselves as others see us is useful.

As you ask the question of need be sure that you ask it imaginatively. Too often, it is asked only in terms of what we know or can find out about our present responsibilities and interests and what our congregations expect of us. But the question What could I become? is fully as important. The Christian Educators Fellowship Conference in 1970 had as its slogan: "You can fly." The conference poster—adapted from one designed at the Grailville Community, Loveland, Ohio—depicted a butterfly leaving its cocoon followed by the words, "but that cocoon has to go." To burst the cocoon requires imagination. Tests and counselors can tell you much about your potentials, but they cannot replace your own imagination. So along the way, fantasize; dream of the lands to which your journey could take you!

2) *What resources are available?* Matching resources to needs is a crucial step in planning. Once you have identified your needs it then remains to find the best resource to meet them. Some of us have not taken that step because we have not known of programs or financial help available. Some of us have not taken it because we were bewildered by all the programs of which we did know (while I am unsure of the reasons, I still find it interesting that in some regions where a wealth of program possibilities exist there are fewer persons engaged in continuing education than in some others where resources are scarcer). Still others of us have taken the wrong step by mismatching needs and resources.

The next chapter is devoted entirely to a survey of resources and how to get more information about them (you may want to read it before continuing). Here I want simply to emphasize the importance of the question and say a bit about how it gets asked.

You do not need *a* continuing education program. You need

55

a *particular* program resource to meet a *particular* need. Matching content needs with resources is relatively easy as long as you are selective in terms of quality. Matching needs with style of program requires more care. Recently I talked with a pastor who has taken considerable responsibility for his own continuing education planning in a region where his denomination has offered little encouragement and no support. He had attended a program at a well-known seminary to which he had traveled several hundred miles. The content matched his strongly felt needs. Much to his disappointment, however, he found himself lectured to for hours on end with almost no chance for discussion. So accustomed had he grown to a dialogical teaching-learning process that the program was more frustrating than helpful.

The very nature of a need will often dictate the style of education called for. For skill development in human relations reading and lectures can be useful, but few major changes will occur without laboratory training in human relations. On the other hand, to study the thought of Teilhard de Chardin requires reading and reflection and can be facilitated by contact with an expert, perhaps in a seminar setting.

We should also give attention to where a resource is available. The classroom concept has conditioned us to think that continuing education is something for which we go to a seminary, a special agency, or some other institution. It is always useful to ask such questions as: Can I get what I need close at hand? Is a study guide available? Could our colleague group use a speakerphone to spend an hour with a specialist many miles away? Is a quality program available nearby which could satisfy the same need as a well-known one a thousand miles away? To some of you accustomed to ask such questions, they may sound elementary. Yet I am amazed at how many times I hear of someone spending hundreds of dollars on transportation with no apparent rationale when a resource of equal value was near at hand.

You may have good reason to travel a long distance for a special program. I am only concerned that in planning you ask the "where" question seriously. When you do spend time and money in travel, it should be for sound reasons.

3) *What are the reality factors?* Time, money, the family, recent or impending job change, program availability—all these modify the ideal plan. Most decisions will be the result of compromise. Sometimes a compromise is unexpectedly productive. Lack of money or a special need to be near one's family may force the search for a resource close at hand which turns out to be more useful than one far away.

Time is a scarce resource for most professionals. Various publics make their demands. Failure to say no when it is appropriate commits us to more time than we have and precipitates anxiety. The mimeographed minutes presented to a meeting I attended recently reported the next meeting set for September 35. The too-loud laughter reflected the group's tension about the time problem. Time is curiously intermixed with our neurotic compulsions: "If I only had enough time, maybe—just maybe—I could satisfy God!"

As professionals we do not have blocks of time naturally available for education. That is part of our reality situation. Organized study is not our primary business, and we need not feel guilty about it. We must stuff some of our study into the spare cracks. The use of cassette players in the automobile, e.g., is rapidly spreading. Why not?

But solid blocks of time are an absolute necessity. To have them requires priority-setting and hard choices. If you are not finding time to continue your education, something is wrong— in your understanding of professional ministry, in your central faith commitments, or in the healthy functioning of your personality. If that sounds judgmental, it is.

Compromise necessitated by reality factors does not always mean delay. If the course in exegesis had been available to Elliot in the fall instead of the spring quarter, the work on societal issues with his colleague group would still have been a first step. Other informal opportunities could have been substituted in the interim, e.g., several extended visits with respected preachers exploring how they practiced their craft.

4) *What is being accomplished?* Education by its nature is intended to produce change. Too often we attend a program, work with a colleague group, read a book, without seriously asking whether we have changed sufficiently to merit the cost. If continuing education is goal-oriented, then we will have something to measure against. Perhaps a major reason that we do not evaluate the effect of our continuing education more often is that we really have no idea what change we expect from it.

MAJOR STEPS IN PLANNING

The following six steps are a basic guide for your planning processes. They will not always be followed in just this order, especially for those who are well underway. They will, however, serve as a reminder of the basic elements in an effective plan.

1) *Begin.* A careful career assessment or an evaluation of your effectiveness or both provides an ideal beginning for a continuing education plan. If an assessment or evaluation is possible, well and good. In that case, step number two becomes step number one. But if they are not immediately available, you need not wait. Take a look at your interests and needs. If possible talk them over with someone who can give you realistic feedback. Then take a first step. Use a study guide, read a book, participate in a seminar, or enroll in a course that looks as if it will address your needs.

But now it will be in a different key from what has gone before. Instead of random choice to participate in a program or read a book, you will be taking the first step of a journey. This opening episode will be felt as part of an unfolding program designed to meet your needs and, in turn, the needs of those whom you serve.

One step may lead easily into another, as with my friend who read *Journey Inward, Journey Outward* and then began a study of the Psalms. You should not go far, however, until you take step two.

2) *Assess needs.* Soon—if it has not been possible at the very beginning, you will want to ask seriously and carefully: What do I need? What are the values, interests, abilities, potentialities, and the like in terms of which I want to develop my career? Where am I in the span of my career? What does my job require in terms of my own perceptions and those of my congregation? Do I want to move into a new kind of ministry or perhaps another occupation entirely? Answers to such questions will give you the data you need to plan effectively.

Almost all of us require help for this kind of careful assessment. It is available in a variety of settings. Elliot, e.g., began a partial assessment of himself in the congregational consultation followed by further clarification in his colleague group, culminating finally in a career assessment at a center.

A career assessment at a career development center or a group assessment led by the staff of a center will enable you to look at these questions in a careful and coherent way and with expert help. Most of us need such an assessment several times during our careers, and when we seriously decide to begin our continuing education or renew it, that offers one of the best occasions.

I recognize that such a career assessment is not always possible or advisable at this point. Fortunately some useful instruments are now available for colleague groups and pastor-parish or comparable committees to use in assessing needs.[5]

Whatever method you use, do not let this step pass. On it everything which follows depends. Note, however, that the question of needs will be asked many times as you plan step 6.

3) *Set goals.* They will be both short- and long-term. To

---

[5] Contact the Academy of Parish Clergy for instruments they have available or suggest. See Appendix I for address.

prepare for a certain kind of job down the road several years is a long-term goal. To engage in the systematic development of a given skill is another. In Elliot's case, the improvement of his preaching was a short-term goal, which led to the development of his capacity to be open to others, a long-range goal. In other words one goal for continuing education is to accomplish something that needs doing soon—anything from improving a skill to preparing adequately to lead a class striving to grasp the content of a significant new book. Others are to be accomplished over a longer period of time and are related closely to long-range career goals.

When we have goals, we then have a basis to establish priorities and make choices. We also have a basis for evaluating our progress (step 5).

4) *Establish a plan.* Assessing needs, setting goals, surveying resources, and acknowledging reality factors are all parts of planning. When they have been cared for, however, the plan itself remains to be devised. Whether done alone or with consultation, this final step is the keystone of the process. To it we now turn. First we shall look at several characteristics of a productive plan and then an example.

Approximately two years is an optimum period to project a plan. Some of the major educational programs must be prepared for that far in advance. Some of the learning goals which we establish require two years to reach. Many of the new D.Min. degrees require at least this period.

To plan in detail beyond two years is difficult. A new job may come along; a strong new personal interest may emerge; a major congregational program may require special preparation. Life and career are sufficiently full of surprises that two years is the advisable limit.

This is not to say that a plan will not project some activities beyond two years. A long-term study leave or sabbatical requires planning far in advance; a D.Min. degree program may extend beyond two years; special activities to help meet the needs of the mid-career or preretirement crises can be anticipated many years ahead. So there are exceptions.

A productive plan is flexible. Some goals set at the beginning may be superceded by others; interests which emerge from a learning project may be so strong that something planned earlier will be set aside. In fact some of the same surprises, which make it difficult to plan for more than two years, require flexibility within the plan itself.

A plan reflects compromises. The reality factors often render ideal choices impossible. You might, for example, establish a career goal to acquire more skill as a family counselor, with a strong desire to train for it immediately. The right training program, however, might not be available near at hand and a study leave impossible for at least a year. In such case compromise is required. But a less urgent goal can be worked at until the other details fall in place.

A plan includes "majors" and "minors." By a "major" I mean a learning project or program of sufficient length and intensity to result in a substantial gain in competence. A major might be a personally planned reading program or one directed through study guides; a semester's course in a nearby school; a five-day human relations lab; an intensive review of Jeremiah's life and prophecy, including exegetical work on the text; the series of studies and projects required in a D.Min. degree program. A major, in other words, is not a quick dip into a subject which only gives one the taste of it. Rather, it is the solid pursuit that gives a new sense of mastery.

One major at any given time is all that the demands of professional practice will allow. As important as education is to our competence, it is not our main business. Education is instrumental to the practice of ministry in lively contact with those whom we serve. And so, taking into account that our learning program will also include "minors," one major pursuit is usually all that we can afford.

A major study at the heart of a learning program carries with it a solid satisfaction which random and occasional study does not provide. Too often we dip into a subject, find it intriguing, but go on to something else before we have any sense of having mastered its central ideas, issues, or skills. This, I believe, is one of the major frustrations encountered in continuing education—perhaps without being realized. Most of us would find great satisfaction in knowing that we had mastered (to the degree of mastery allowed a generalist) two to four subject or skill areas each year. In no small measure, the satisfaction springs from a sense of growing competence.

This is no plea for compulsively mastering everything we touch. It is rather recognition of what Peter Drucker describes as "the thrill of finding something, of thinking something through, of truly learning something." [6]

A program will also need to allow for "minors" most of which will not be planned far in advance. Some will occur quite by surprise. You will see a book with an intriguing title; you will decide to preach a sermon which requires special study and research; a periodical or cassette tape arrives. Elliot's listening to the cassette at the end of his plan probably seemed discontinuous with what had gone before. It was. Our continuing education will always include minors not integrally connected to its major themes and projects.

You who are women confront a special set of needs which will affect your planning—or so it seems to me as a man. These needs arise from the growing awareness that the woman must struggle for full liberation in a male-oriented society and profession. A number of women, recognizing this situation, now realize that they face a basic choice in continuing education planning: whether to stick it out in male-planned and -dominated programs and groups or whether to devote their primary time and energy to participation in and creation of programs and

[6] Peter F. Drucker, "The University in an Educated Society," in *The Oakland Papers*, James B. Whipple and Cary A. Woditsch, eds. (Boston: CSLEA, 1966), p. 15.

groups by and for women. And creation it will be in many cases, since the program resources currently available especially for women are often of high quality but few and far between.

A Two-Year Plan

(The plan devised by Elliot soon after his career assessment, building, in part, upon goals set at that time.)

Majors	Minors
First year	Continuing activities through both years:
January-March: Colleague group use of Perkins Study Guide, "Exegesis of a N.T. Gospel: Mark" (including one-day closing seminar with N.T. professor).	Colleague group, except summers. Use of audio and print periodicals. Reading books of special interest. Study required for sermon preparation and teaching.
April (post-Easter): Human relations seminar (five days, requiring short study leave).	Special activities anticipated during first year.
May-July: Reading program in human relations and personal growth (planned with help of seminar leader, local seminary professor and colleague group).	*January-March:* Preparation for new youth membership training program in cooperation with two local pastors.
August: Vacation.	*April-June:* Colleague group weekly case study project.
September-December: Course at nearby seminary: Contemporary thought about Jesus.	*October-December:* Preparation for Advent sermons on the Messiah, building upon seminary class on Jesus.
Second year	Second year
January-March: Personal preparation to lead congregational Lenten study, "The	Plans for special activites to be developed late in first year and early in second.

Church's Response to a Suf-
fering World."

April-July: Reading program of contemporary
novels and drama (to be
planned during March).

August: Vacation.
September: Participation,
annual four-day judicatory
seminar.

October-December: No
major study in lieu of preparation for three-month
leave (January-March) for
study of experiential theology and its relation to
preaching.

5) *Plan for a major study leave or sabbatical.* A long-term
leave or sabbatical planned well in advance and designed to
meet definite learning and career goals should be part of your
plan. Three to nine months of concentrated work on one or
two areas of interest can enrich your practice of ministry for
years ahead. Many judicatories now provide support for long-
term leaves, and many church professionals are finding that they
can look forward to several during their careers.

That a long-term leave takes careful advance planning goes
virtually without saying.

6) *Reevaluate personal and professional growth and reassess
needs.* "What happened to me—really?" is a question seldom
asked by participants in continuing education episodes of any
kind. We may sense how we felt about the experience; we may
know our reaction to a speaker or an author. But we seldom
stop, I fear, and ask what we really learned from an experience
which will enhance our growth in personhood and in profes-

64

sional competence. The failure is regrettable. It lets valuable learning dissipate.

I would strongly encourage you to spend at least several hours after significant learning episodes, reflecting on their usefulness and directly relating your learnings to your life and work. It will be time well spent. I would also urge a colleague group to apply its ingenuity to evaluation and integration of learnings at the close of each major project.

In this final step I also include the reassessment of needs. The initial evaluation or assessment of your career and your work will provide data for your initial planning. But at many other times in the course of your career you will need to take a careful look at yourself and your work in order to modify your goals or set new ones and make appropriate choices of your majors.

One of the most encouraging current developments is the increasing attention being given by the Academy of Parish Clergy, denominational judicatories, and other groups to the creation of instruments and procedures for evaluation. We can look for an increasing number of instruments and suggested procedures to assist us in this task.

THE STUDY LEAVE

Even though the basic fare of continuing education is the learning which occurs at home base, there will be times when leaving home for a continuing education program will be useful. It is likely that many short study leaves and several long ones will be included in your plan over the years.

But you do not take a study leave just to be taking one—not if you are serious about your continuing education. As with all elements in your plan, a study leave will be designed to meet your goals, adjusted to the reality factors, and fitted into the total design.

There is no best or standard length. Recently I heard a group of ministers discuss whether a year or six months or three, is the best length for a long-term leave. Their discussion missed the point. The right length is that which you need to meet your goals modified by the reality factors.

Having said that, I would surmise that for most of us a short leave of three to ten days, once a year, might be both appropriate and possible. In some years, however, it might not be appropriate at all, e.g., if you are enrolled in a course; in other years, two short leaves might be called for. The point is that the decision to engage in a study leave be tailored to your plan, not vice versa.

What values does the short leave have in contrast to study near home base? They are quite obvious, but let me list them briefly: (1) cross-fertilization of ideas with persons beyond your local community; (2) short but intensive contact with one or more specialists; (3) a break with routine; (4) the fellowship-in-learning values which inhere especially in programs such as the United Methodist Pastors Schools planned for the ministers of a given judicatory.

The long-term leave and sabbatical. The primary function of such leaves is to make a major advance in one or two areas of competence, an advance that would be difficult without periods of concentrated work free from the distraction of daily routine. It also allows for personal renewal, both in terms of new perspectives on one's life and work and the enrichment which multiple opportunities for participation in cultural events, special short seminars, and the like afford.

In 1971 I took a study leave of four months, three of which were spent at Harvard. My primary goal was to gain a rudimentary understanding of ego, or personality development theory. One of my long-range learning goals is to acquire specialized knowledge of career development, particularly in relation to ministry. That, I had realized, would require a basic understanding of how we develop as human beings, especially as adults. I had opportunity to read for eight to ten hours a day under the guidance of a professor. I audited several classes, including classes at the Graduate School of Business and the Divinity School. I heard special lectures, attended forums, concerts, plays, movies. It was a rich experience.

During the leave I was able to erect a framework of knowledge upon which I can continue to build in years to come and which will provide useful tools for my work. The deep satisfaction which has accompanied this process has confirmed my belief about the human drive for competence. There were significant additional benefits. One had to do with my ability to think imaginatively about myself and my work. To relax my daily-responsibility mind-set took some time. Once that happened, I found that spontaneously I was reflecting imaginatively upon my work: its goals; its relation to my personal life and my family; its priorities; its methodology. Another benefit was the broadening of mind and spirit which came from new friendships and the multitude of special events in which I participated. I would covet for every professional church leader a similar opportunity at least twice in a career.

We are, I believe, rapidly approaching the time when that will be a possibility for many. The one-year leave, or sabbatical, may continue to be possible for a relatively small number, but special support arrangements now being devised by many local and national judicatories will put the three-to-six-month leave within the reach of many.

THE PROFESSIONAL DOCTORATE

At a meeting of theological school representatives and other church leaders in the early summer of 1973 Dr. Marvin J. Taylor reported that 60 percent of the accredited Protestant seminaries in the United States are either offering, or have definite plans to offer, a doctor of ministry degree. These degrees are progeny (often with mixed blood) of the professional doctor's and master's degrees initiated by San Francisco Theological Seminary in the early 1960s. They break, or claim to break, with the more traditional doctorates in their focus on the professional responsibilities rather than on traditional subject areas of the liberal arts and sciences degree.

Without question more seminaries will offer D.Min. degrees before the number levels off, and the number of church professionals enrolling will increase. Since this kind of degree program is one method of planning a several-year span of continuing education, this is an appropriate point to look briefly at these degrees as continuing education.[7]

The D.Min. has several potential values as continuing education: (1) It provides a form of guidance for need assessment, goal-setting, and designing an appropriate sequence of learning events; (2) it takes professional practice seriously both in terms of its use as a datum for learning and its enhanced effectiveness as an outcome; (3) it helps build continuing education into the daily routine of work.

The D.Min. also has limitations: (1) Its primary lure can be increased status rather than solid advance in competence to be continued once the degree is complete; (2) once in the program, one has less freedom for alternate choices of learning resources until the degree is complete; (3) unless the degree program has been imaginatively designed and breaks markedly, if not radically, with more traditional degree programs, it can be merely a return to the study of more-or-less discreet subject areas without relating them to the tasks of professional life; (4) it is expensive.

For some, the D.Min. is well suited; for others, not. Allow

[7] Our concern here is with the in-ministry form of the D.Min. programs, not with the in-sequence form in which the D.Min. is essentially an extension of basic degree preparation for professional practice.

me to suggest several questions which you might ask yourself and the sponsoring school:

1) What personal-professional goals will the program fulfill? Or, if my goals are unclear, does the degree provide a career assessment which will assist me in clarification?

2) Is the cost in time, family life, money, worth the potential value in contrast to other possibilities?

3) What pattern of career assessment is built into the program, especially at its beginning? (I believe that a career assessment is a necessary part of such programs, and I do not mean a battery of tests and several interviews labeled career assessment. I mean an assessment by properly trained and accredited personnel.)

4) Is the program genuinely professionally oriented? All D.Mins. claim to be; not all are. Some are cosmetically rouged traditional programs.

5) Does the plan provide for work with and/or supervision by practicing professionals who are themselves under rigorous training? This, I believe, is an absolute essential. Professors will have their important role, but a professional doctorate without *serious* and *substantial* involvement of practitioners as teachers is a sure sign of a painted-over traditional degree.

6) Does the program provide a means to project your career and learning goals beyond the degree program? Does the program help you design study into your daily routine and learn how to reflect creatively on your practice of ministry? I am leery of those programs which require a majority of the class and other work in residence. The requirement diverts attention from the relation of education to daily professional work.

From the foregoing one could get the impression that I see no place for a Ph.D. or similar degree program in continuing education. I do, but as a rare exception. If a Ph.D. degree has been started after seminary but left unfinished, its completion can sometimes be useful, though I have seen it exact terrible costs in time and family life without appropriate benefit in increased competence. A Ph.D. is sometimes appropriate when one decides to make career change early in a career. Because its design is suited primarily to academe, I would think that for the church professional, planning to continue in that role, to begin a Ph.D. would almost never be appropriate. (To what rule, however, is there not an exception?)

Integrally linked to planning is the discovery and appropriation of resources. To that we now turn.

Chapter V

RESOURCES

𝔗𝔥𝔢 𝔘𝔫𝔦𝔱𝔢𝔡 𝔐𝔢𝔱𝔥𝔬𝔡𝔦𝔰𝔱 ℭ𝔥𝔲𝔯𝔠𝔥
DAVID FRAIN, PASTOR
RICHARDSON AVE. AND NORTH FOURTH ST.
ASHTON, ILLINOIS 61006

The resources for continuing education are vast, but that very fact is bewildering. I have long felt that a highly useful tool for planning would be a classification of the groups, agencies, schools, and other institutions which provide resources and some clues about how to get specific information. This chapter is intended to be such a tool. It addresses two major questions: 1) To what kinds of agencies do I look for programs, financial help, and other resources? 2) How do I get specific information?

Before looking at the external resources available, look for a moment at the primary resource at your disposal—your own mind. It is at once the richest and most essential resource. Whether or not the other resources have value, depends upon the degree to which you utilize your own mind in appropriating them. An idea enters your mind from a book, a lecturer, or a colleague. It may be a significant idea, but if your mind does not examine it, play with it and, finally, incorporate it into your mental schema, it is essentially lost. How often I catch myself, and observe others, assuming that if we only read enough, hear enough, see enough we will be educated without tapping our own mental powers. One key idea, carefully examined through one day, is more educative than a book or a lecture absorbed, but unexamined. Furthermore, our minds subconsciously hold stored a wealth of ideas and impressions which are at our disposal when we find ways to release them into consciousness.

Two basic kinds of resources are available; program and support. I use "program" in a broad sense. By it I mean such things as seminars, classes, colleague groups, as well as materials and media. By support resources I mean those which we can draw upon for help to plan and carry out our continuing education program.

PROGRAM RESOURCES

Program resources fall into three categories:

I. Resources available at home
  Colleague groups
  Personal library
  Library loan services and guided study
  Telephone, television, film
  Continuing courses, seminars, etc.
II. Short-term programs away from home sponsored by
  Denominational and interdenominational agencies
  Educational institutions
    Seminaries
    Colleges and universities
  Specialized agencies
  Programs by and for women
III. Resources for the long-term study leave and sabbatical

Resources available at home. Until the late 1960s continuing education was viewed predominantly as something to be done away from home. In those years, however, the concept gradually gained ground that the foundation of continuing education is what happens within daily and weekly professional activity—at home. Within the first years of the 1970s the spread of the concept has increased exponentially. We are now virtually in a new period. This being so, the primary resources for continuing education are those which you can utilize at home. Programs for which you must leave home remain important and can be formative, but are secondary.

1) Colleague groups. Perhaps the most important resource for your continuing education is the one most frequently overlooked—a group of colleagues in ministry.

To think of a colleague group as a resource instead of a setting for continuing education may be surprising. It is, of course, a setting and potentially one of the best, but resource it is also. Examination of shared ideas and experiences of colleagues, especially when brought to the group in case-study form, is productive in a degree very difficult to achieve alone or in one-to-one conversation. Group dialogue produces syntheses through the tugs and pulls of opposing ideas and insights. At other times, ideas build rapidly upon one another, resulting in surprising new constructs.

Not least important among the resources of a group are the accountability and sense of support (two sides of the same coin) for continuing disciplined learning.

So important is the colleague group to the entire enterprise that I have devoted a later chapter to it.

2) Personal libraries. Library-building is a major task in continuing education. We have limited money to spend, and to use it wisely takes careful thought. Inevitably, we will buy books which are interesting and timely but soon outdated. The problem lies in spending so much that way (many such books can be borrowed) that we will not build a library of standard works to have at our fingertips when we need them. One of my early pastorates was a church across the street from a college library. Soon after I moved away I realized my overdependence. I was appalled to see the outdated books on my shelves and the absence of standard works. Connolly Gamble gives this wise counsel about a personal library.

Home study is essential. Here is where the minister has more time available than any other place that could be conceived

73

as his center for continuing education. Here he and his fellow churchmen may create a learning laboratory in their own community, where ministers and laymen teach and learn together in fruitful interchange. . . . In home study *a primary resource,* whether for an individual or a small group, *is the collection of books, and other materials which are gathered into private libraries.* Continuing education is based upon a well-planned personal library.[1] (italics mine)

Materials—lectures, clinical materials for the practice of ministry, books—are now available on audio cassette tapes. Perhaps even more caution is necessary in their purchase than in print materials. A tape can become dated just as soon as a book; it takes longer to hear material than to read it; scanning is all but impossible; sections for future use are more difficult to get at. This is not to say that tapes should not be purchased; it is only to counsel caution.

A personal library also includes carefully chosen print and audio periodicals, the selective reading and hearing of which is one of the competence-producing minors.

A particular kind of periodical, the digest, is one means of coping with the knowledge explosion and the rapid tempo of events. It is virtually impossible to keep in touch adequately entirely through original sources. Busy professionals in all fields are turning without apology to digests whose editors scan, select, and edit from vast materials in given fields.

In this day of their precarious existence, I hesitate to mention periodicals specifically. Reference to two, however, will illustrate the type of digest periodicals useful to professional church leaders: *Context: A Commentary on the Interaction of Religion and Culture,* written by Martin E. Marty and published fortnightly by the Thomas More Association. In six concisely written pages, *Context* compresses remarkably the current ideas, moods,

---

[1] "Short Term Programs of Continuing Education," in *The Continuing Quest,* James B. Hofrenning, ed. (Minneapolis: Augsburg Press, 1970), p. 69.

and movements in its defined area. Marty scans, selects, and condenses a vast amount of materials. With a minimum of reading one is in touch with a broad range of materials and finds clues for further investigation.

Thesis Theological Cassettes, an audio tape periodical published by the Thesis Educational Resources. Selections are made from dozens of recorded lectures and interviews for a monthly one-hour tape. The voices of leading scholars and practicing professionals in ministry, carefully edited, provide maximum idea content in a short time. Audio periodicals are sufficiently expensive that some cannot afford them individually. Several persons subscribing jointly put their cost within reach.

3) Library loan services and study guides. More conventional but highly useful in this category is the loan of individual books. Three types of libraries are available in addition to the public libraries. (Public libraries are sometimes not thought of as major continuing education resources, but in cities of any size they are.) (1) Privately endowed libraries. Two in New England—Zion Research and General Theological—send books all over the United States. Several well-endowed extension libraries especially for professionals in the church are located at seminaries, such as the Jordan Loan Library at Duke. Most of these libraries regularly send out lists of new accessions and bibliographies on given subjects. (2) Seminary libraries which increasingly are encouraging extension use as part of their continuing education programs. (3) State university libraries which offer extension privileges. Many have excellent religious collections.

A number of libraries (including a growing number at seminaries) have tape collections for loan. One major library established exclusively for loan of tapes on religious subjects is the Reigner Library, Union Theological Seminary, Richmond, Virginia. Another is at the School of Theology at Claremont in California.

Guided study provides one of the most useful resources currently available. Within the last decade approximately twelve thousand clergy and laity have followed their continuing education through one of the seminary guided study programs. The study guides to which I refer are short (usually eight to ten pages) outline studies of a given subject using the most up-to-date materials available. Upon enrollment, you receive the guide and first set of study materials (books, articles, sometimes cassette tapes). The material is gauged to approximately what can be covered within two weeks. You return the first set and the second is sent to you and so on until the study is finished (usually six to eight units). Enrollment in some guides is free. Others require a small service charge.

Perkins School of Theology through the leadership of Richard Murray, Director of Continuing Education, has pioneered group use of guided study. At the end of a study a group of at least ten persons can have, without honorarium cost, a one-day seminar with a specialist in the subject of the guide used. A network of schools has joined Perkins in this guided study service and at the time of this writing the United Methodist Division of Ordained Ministry has inaugurated an experimental system called New Dimensions which makes this kind of resource available to individuals and groups anywhere in the United States.

A study guide answers two basic questions for the busy professional: (1) What are the most up-to-date and useful materials in an area of my interest? (2) In what order should they be studied? It also responds to two motivational factors in our continuing education: First, accessibility; bringing major resources to us where we are. Second, accountability. If used by a group, members help hold one another responsible for study.

4) Telephone, television, and film. A number of states now have telephone continuing education networks (sometimes linked with closed circuit TV) sponsored by hospital associations and regional medical programs and also by state university extension or continuing education systems. In Tennessee, for

example, approximately 125 hospitals are linked in four networks with sophisticated new speakerphones in conference hospital rooms. Each week some six hundred to two thousand persons, ranging from doctors to dietitians, participate in lecture-discussion programs. Everyone can hear what is said—including questions, reports, points of view—by anyone else in any hospital linked to a particular session. In some regions there are established programs for church leaders using these networks; in others, experimental programs are being planned.

A system may exist in your own state only waiting to be used. Universities and health organizations are cordial to use of their networks by church groups. With relatively small cost per person, you can have conversation on religious subjects and many secular ones with almost any specialist in the United States. If no such system now exists near you, your own initiative can create one.

Installation and monthly rental costs are modest. A church in your vicinity would perhaps see the value of a speakerphone in its adult education program and split the installation and rental costs with your ministerial association or other group. In 1973 the rate for a one-hour evening call from St. Louis to Atlanta station-to-station was approximately twelve dollars plus tax. Add to that a twenty-five dollar honorarium, and for a group of ten to fifteen, that is relatively inexpensive continuing education when compared to the cost of a leader's being brought to your group or your attending a program in another city.

National Educational Television stations carry programs which blanket the United States. The use of cable TV for educational purposes is just on the horizon. Both of these visual electronic media have a limited present usefulness but high potential. We should not, however, overrate the value of a picture in front of us in educational programs. Some studies now show that learning can be just as high from pure audio communication as from video, unless special reason exists to depict something.

Movies are available everywhere, and many have high educational potential. In *Sunday Night at the Movies,*[2] Dr. G. William Jones of Southern Methodist University has helped us realize the educational usefulness of movies which many had thought of as entertainment only. Many film libraries make available a wide range of movies at moderate costs.

5) Continuing classes, seminars, etc. Except in some regions of the West, few of us live beyond commuting distance from colleges, universities, clinical pastoral education agencies, urban training units, or other educational/training agencies. These offer a wide variety of programs with weekly or more frequent sessions extended over a semester, quarter, or other period. They thus provide opportunity for long-term continuing education without leaving home.

Appropriately included here are the increasing number of programs sponsored by seminaries which send professors out to hold weekly or monthly classes, sometimes for credit, with groups meeting close to their homes. Two outstanding examples are CHARIS, based at Concordia College, which sponsors credit courses in local communities throughout northern Minnesota and eastern North and South Dakota, and the Academy of Theological Studies program of the School of Theology at Claremont, which conducts courses locally throughout the West Coast region.

Short-term programs away from home. There are three kinds of agencies sponsoring such programs:

1) Denominational and interdenominational groups. Most major denominations now have national offices with full- or part-time responsibility for continuing education.[3] Rapidly local judicatories—annual conferences, dioceses, presbyteries—are establishing continuing education committees. These national and local bodies are primary sponsors of continuing education programs. In The United Methodist Church each year more than

[2] (Richmond, Va.: John Knox Press, 1967).
[3] Cf. Appendix I.

150 programs are planned by annual conference agencies. Forty of these are in a related system of short, three- to five-day institutes, many of which are known as pastors schools, some having a history of more than a half century. They offer a wide variety of programs.

My experience with programs sponsored by local judicatories is that they are often remarkably effective. Sometimes they are lacking in educational sophistication, but that is improving. Their major strength lies in their being planned by professionals for fellow professionals. Increasingly, the planners are attempting to sense the felt needs of potential participants.

One of the most significant developments in programming by local judicatories is their inclusion of continuing education within the broader context of career development. Programs are now being planned related to major career change or crisis periods.

The trend is away from national denominational bodies' being sole sponsors of continuing education programs. Increasingly they provide back-up services to their local judicatories and educational agencies as program producers. Nevertheless, they still offer high quality programs such as the Young Pastors Program of The United Presbyterian Church in the U.S.A. and programs related to the particular interests of a national agency. For example, world mission boards sponsor travel seminars focusing on the church's work overseas. Several denominations sponsor programs at the Church Center for the United Nations in New York city. An inquiry to a national agency can quickly uncover the programs offered.

The trend within the last five years has been away from programs sponsored by interdenominational agencies, partially because of waning support for councils of churches. Some strong interdenominational programs remain, especially in the form of statewide annual conferences for ministers, with outstanding lecturers and other leaders.

2) Educational institutions. This section refers to the pro-

grams offered by the more traditional degree-granting, educational institutions in our society. They fall naturally into two groups: (1) schools of theology; (2) colleges and universities. In a preceding section, we discussed the possibility of regular participation in classes or training programs for those living near these institutions. Here we will focus on short-term residential programs.

First, schools of theology. Long before the term came into vogue, schools of theology offered courses and programs with a view to the minister's continuing education. One has only to think of the Union Theological Seminary (New York) Summer School which for decades has drawn professionals from all over the United States.

A wide variety of short-term programs are offered by seminaries, ranging from courses in human relations training to those which focus on biblical and theological subjects. Increasingly, they take the personal-professional issues and concerns of the minister as a point of departure. Far less than formerly are they designed as return-to-seminary programs planned to update one in the latest developments in a given field. Nevertheless, when selecting a program one should be cautious of the latter. As adults, the concerns arising from our lives—including our work—are a major motivational factor for genuine learning. Dr. Robert Reber is correct in saying: "Significant learning (for adults) takes place when the learner perceives that the subject matter, or problem to be considered is relevant to *his own purposes* and has *personal meaning for him*. If this is not the case, the learner will hardly be motivated to give energy and direction to his learning." [4] We may be intrigued by the prospect of discovering the latest development in a given field, only to find that we have little interest once we are involved.

Generally speaking, seminaries offer continuing education

[4] Robert E. Reber, "The World Council of Churches and World Development: Proposals for Adult Education in the Churches," (Ph.D. diss., Boston University, 1973), p. 205 (italics mine).

programs at two periods: (1) in summer schools which in some cases are designed, totally or in major part, for the practicing professional, and are usually broken into two-week segments allowing for variety of time-involvement; (2) during the regular academic year, sometimes during a one-month inter-term. Those several schools which have special residential facilities (e.g., Princeton, Saint Paul School of Theology, Union in Richmond) or which have nearby facilities available have much more leeway than others in residential program development.

Seminaries are now offering short-term residential programs which are integral to the doctor of ministry degree programs.

The primary program resource offered by colleges and universities has already been discussed in terms of the opportunity for those nearby to enroll in their regular courses. Their short-term program opportunities are much more limited but are sufficiently frequent to merit attention.

Church-related colleges occasionally sponsor short-term programs, usually for ministers in their vicinity. Several have established centers or ongoing programs, e.g., the Continuing Education Center at Rocky Mountain College, Billings, Montana, and the program designed especially for United Methodist lay pastors at West Virginia Wesleyan. I would judge that programs offered by church-related schools will increase.

The major short-term program of the university traditionally has been offered through the extension programs of the land grant universities. For many years these programs were planned annually primarily with the small town and rural church in mind. They have provided a far more valuable service than many realize. For a long while the focus was on enabling the pastor to understand the sociology of rural life, how it affects the church and the church affects it. This focus remains for some programs. Now, however, with the boundaries between rural and urban becoming less distinct, these programs, still with the rural and small town church in view, are shifting their focus to social change.[5] Several university extension agencies offer annual programs which are attracting nationwide attention and draw participants from a region beyond their own state, e.g., the Appalachian Regional School for Church Leaders at the West Virginia University in Morgantown; and the Great Plains Church Leadership School at Colorado State University, Fort Collins.

Several years ago, the Graduate School of Business at American University established a degree program in church management. In addition it has offered a number of short-term programs. This program pioneered by Dr. Clyde Humphrey has been followed by other graduate schools of business and management, which offer short-term programs for members of our profession or make their services available for establishing programs. The Management for Ministry program at the University of Texas, sponsored jointly by the School of Business and a group of Texas seminaries, is one example.

3) Specialized agencies. A broad range of highly diverse agencies exist whose educational/training programs are focused in one, or several, related areas. Some have attracted a nationwide, others a local, clientele.

Some are independent, existing only for education or training; some, such as clinical training programs at hospitals, are part of larger enterprises. Some cater almost entirely to church professionals; some cater to them along with other groups; still others are open to church professionals, but exist primarily for other groups.

Among those specialized agencies which devote their resources primarily to a church clientele, several bear special mention.

Since its founding in 1957 by Dr. Reuel L. Howe, the Institute for Advanced Pastoral Studies, Bloomfield Hills, Michigan,

---

[5] For information about a program in your state land grant university, write the U.S. Department of Agriculture, Federal Extension Service, Washington, D.C. 20250.

has pioneered in continuing education in an ecumenical setting. Using seasoned and imaginative leaders, it has shaped a variety of programs to provide help for ministers and lay persons facing the problems and changes of the contemporary world. Under the leadership of its new director, Dr. John E. Biersdorf, some of these programs will continue, and new programs for the future of the institute will be tested using multimedia resources, research documentation, and new training designs.

Interpreters' House at Lake Junaluska, North Carolina, under the leadership of Dr. Carlyle Marney, has since 1966 provided programs centering in a basic three-week seminar designed to enable the recovery of and means for continued growth in personhood. Dr. Marney and those working with him have assumed, and rightly, that if personhood is smothered, authentic ministry is impossible.

As of this writing three seminaries which at one time were degree-granting institutions have moved a major portion of their resources into continuing education for church professional leadership and laity:[6] Auburn Theological Seminary, closely related to Union in New York city, was the first to make this change. Several years ago it shifted its program resources to provide help to groups of professionals and laity engaged in continuing education in the field. New York Theological Seminary moved recently from being primarily a degree-granting institution to one which offers both a special semester to students from other schools and continuing education programs for professional church leaders and laity.

The latest school to shift fundamentally the use of its resources for ministry is the Hartford Seminary Foundation. It will provide resources for research in ministry; consultation for

[6] For our purposes here, these may be considered as essentially independent specialized agencies. Their programs are not, for the most part, short-term and residential. This section, however, is the best place to consider them.

parish development and continuing education for professional church leaders. Some programs will be residential, but the bulk of its programming will be with laity and professionals in the field.

The largest single group of specialized agencies are those whose programs focus, in some way, on personal development and human relations. Pioneers in this field are the clinical pastoral education programs which are hospital based and usually an integral part of the hospital's program. Their major function historically has been to prepare persons for chaplaincy careers and, in many cases, to augment basic seminary degree programs.

Gradually, Clinical Pastoral Education (CPE) agencies have broadened their focus. Many have added programs which use the parish instead of the hospital as laboratory. Consequently, they are attracting increasing numbers of pastors as clients. Of immediate interest here is the growing list of those which offer short-term programs, even though their major emphasis continues to be a weekly program for persons living nearby.[7] While the work of the pastor totally or in its several parts may be the concern of the newer CPE programs, the issues of human relations, personal identity, and adequacy remain central.

Programs focused on personal growth and development and human relations per se have increased rapidly in recent years. They cater to a diverse clientele, of which church professionals are a major segment. To locate this kind of program in a particular agency is difficult because sponsorship varies: seminaries, denominational programs, hospital CPE programs. There are, however, several major kinds of agencies for which these programs are a specialty.

Several groups of them are linked in loosely knit networks, partly through having their staffs or leaders certified by national organizations. Until recently, the best-known to many has been

[7] Cf. Appendix I for the address of the Association of Clinical Pastoral Education.

the National Training Laboratories (NTL).[8] The T-group has become the popular symbol of the movement, with sensitivity training as the characteristic descriptive phrase.

> Sensitivity training is one type of experience-based learning. Participants work together in a small group over an extended period of time, learning through analysis of their own experiences, including feelings, reactions, perceptions, and behavior. The sensitivity training group may stand by itself or be part of a larger laboratory training design which might include role playing, case studies, theory presentations, and intergroup exercises.[9]

Programs related to NTL have taken two major directions: (1) organizational development in which the major concerns are to improve one's ability to work with an organization and to help organizations plan; (2) personal development, with the emphasis on enabling the individual to reach his or her full potential. Anyone considering involvement in sensitivity training should find out which emphasis is paramount and how well it matches one's individual needs.[10]

Within recent years a related, but distinct, movement has grown up providing programs in which the primary concern is, personal human development per se. Relationships with other persons figure largely, but are instrumental to discovering and actualizing one's own potential. The human potential movement is, in fact, its broadest descriptive term. Within the movement are several more-or-less closely knit networks of certified trainers. One of the most popular is Transactional Analysis (TA). For

[8] Cf. Appendix I for the address.

[9] "What Is Sensitivity Training?" *NTL Institute News and Reports,* Vol. 2, No. 2, April 1968.

[10] A well-balanced and exceptionally helpful booklet for those who are considering sensitivity training or involvement in encounter groups, is Elizabeth Ogg, *Sensitivity Training and Encounter Groups* (New York: Public Affairs Committee, 1972). It will probably please neither doctrinaire critics nor advocates. To order, write Public Affairs Pamphlets, 381 Park Avenue South, New York, New York 10016.

many weeks its best-known book *I'm OK, You're OK* was the number one nonfiction best seller.[11] This TA training method is grounded in the hypothesis that the mind operates always from one or more of three ego states: parent, child, adult. All personal awareness and all relationships (transactions) arise out of one of these three, singly or in combination. Its training draws heavily also upon Gestalt psychology.

Gestalt psychology is the most pervasive theory and provides the most widely used techniques of the human potential movement. In its earliest stages the fountainhead of this part of the human potential movement was the Esalen Institute at Big Sur, California, which has sponsored an astonishingly wide variety of short-term programs. More recently, Esalen has assumed less relative importance as the movement has spread.[12]

In most cities there are now agencies which sponsor programs focused on personal development and human relations. We have already mentioned CPE programs in hospitals and that seminaries often include such programs in their offerings. Increasingly, one finds centers which specialize in these programs, some church-related, some not. Community mental health centers are one major type of the latter.

Another network of specialized agencies are the Action-Training Centers (many, originally called urban training cen-

[11] Thomas A. Harris (New York: Harper & Row, 1969).
[12] The entire human relations/human potential movement, including its training programs has been strongly defended by its proponents and sharply attacked by its critics. As an example of the latter, cf. Kurt W. Back, "The Group Can Comfort but Can't Cure," *Psychology Today,* 6 (December 1972), 28-29. A substantial amount of self-critique is occurring from within the movement. Especially interesting because of its comparisons of contemporary groups to other small group movements in Christian history is Thomas C. Oden, *The Intensive Group Experience* (Philadelphia: Westminster Press, 1972). Dr. Oden both affirms the values of the intensive group and sharply criticizes it. For anyone considering participation in such groups, the two most important considerations are personal emotional stability (the short-term group experience is, in my judgment, risky as therapy) and the qualification of the leader (certification by a nationally responsible group is a must).

ters[13]). In the 1960s the United States became acutely aware of the urban crisis. As part of the church's response a group of training centers were established to help both clergy and laity to respond in mission to the crisis. In the 1970s concern for the urban crisis per se has turned to other things, or simply waned, causing diminishing financial support for Action-Training Centers. Because of this and other dynamics, their program emphases have broadened, although training for response to the urban crisis remains as a strong component.[14]

To meet what training needs does one turn to an Action-Training Center? Still, primarily, needs related to the urban crisis (which has subsided little even though our attention has been diverted). Secondly, to meet more general needs, provided that a given center offers special programs responsive to them.

The Action-Training Centers utilize a distinctive educational method. Whatever the future of the centers, they have left a valuable legacy. Their leaders in the 1960s pioneered the method now identified in their name—action-training. The basic principle is that education and training for the church's mission cannot be separated from planned involvement in that mission. "If the church's mission is to respond to the world's hurt, how can that mission be reflected upon theologically if the hurt is only remotely known and not personally encountered?" That question is the method's basic presupposition.

Action-reflection was not altogether new to the 1960s or to urban training. The Association for Clinical Pastoral Education has long used it, although it was seldom referred to as such. The Action-Training Centers, however, gave the method new impetus and demonstrated, not just its usefulness, but its necessity in education for mission. The result is that the action-reflection style has permeated education for ministry (though

[13] Cf. Appendix I for the address of the Action-Training Coalition.
[14] J. Alan Winter, Edgar W. Mills, et al. *Clergy in Action Training: A Research Report* (New York: IDOC and the Ministry Studies Board, 1971), reports study of five centers. Chapter 5, "Summary and Implications," is a helpful interpretation of the action-training method.

still insufficiently). There are those now who turn to Action-Training Centers where possible for their continuing education because they want to be involved in programs where the method is used.

These categories do not exhaust the specialized programs and program agencies which provide resources for continuing education. International travel seminars, programs in church family financial planning, alcohol studies, training in management skills, are available, many of them sponsored by agencies established and funded for those purposes, some offered by universities, seminaries, and other agencies with broader purposes. The fact is that scarcely any need of church professionals can now be identified for which there is not some program or program agency available. The question is: How can they be located? To that we shall turn shortly.

4) Programs especially for women. A growing need exists today for continuing education programs and program resources planned by and for women with their needs and concerns primarily in view. Too many times programs planned predominantly *by* men turn out to be *for* men.

But the need also has a strong positive rationale. In a milieu of rising women's consciousness and in the face of resistance to their assuming a full place in ministry, women need opportunities for their own learning experiences in which support, strategy formation, and growth in personal awareness are intermixed with cognitive learning.

A few such programs and program resources now exist, but very few. Some of those listed below are available—at least at this writing. They are described, in part, however, to indicate the resources which women have created and can create in cooperation with schools and agencies concerned for liberating education.

Held in the fall of 1971, sponsored by the Graduate Theological Union, "Women and the Word—Toward a Whole Theology" was a course which enrolled women of all ages and relationships to the church. Requested by women of three semi-naries, its educational style was set by them. It was characterized by learning based on sharing within the group; sharing with women in the surrounding community; use of resource persons as catalysts.

Church Employed Women and the Menninger Foundation have jointly sponsored a therapeutic seminar for clergywomen. "The focus was on the internal stress which results from pressures, discrimination and disillusionments women meet while attempting to serve the church and survive in a male-dominated culture." [15]

The Grail is an organization composed until recently entirely of Roman Catholic women. Founded in Belgium after World War I, it now has houses and centers in eleven countries. Grailville, its national conference center in Loveland, Ohio, sponsors, among other things, an educational program for women. For several years the annual Grailville Conference has been an intense experience for lay and professional women. Workshops are the basis of the week's program. Formed as a result of group deliberation, the workshops have had no leaders or convenors, but have been self-run. "Everyone participated in the theologizing; distinctions between 'professional' theologians and those without similar training were simply not important because every woman brought with her 'live' theological data from her own religious experience and her experiences as a woman." [16]

Programs and materials developed by United Methodist Women and other national denominational agencies are increasingly devoted to women's concerns. The 1973–74 study, *Women: Over Half the Earth's People,* sponsored by The United Methodist Church, is an excellent resource. Adjunct to that study

[15] From a description of this program written by Betty Strathman Pagett to whom I am indebted for much of the program information in this section.

[16] *Report on Grailville* (New York: Church Women United, 1972).

is "Women: Perspectives on a Movement," available both as a set of study materials and as a guided study.[17]

Two women's groups were funded by Auburn Theological Seminary in 1970-71. One of these comprised six women dispersed in three cities; meeting together every two months, but who communicated between times through letters, phone calls, and in subgroups of twos and threes. Betty Pagett who was a member of the group says, "I can attest to its skill development for me as we set our own agenda analyzing the impact of the Judaeo-Christian tradition on women."

Continuing education for women has been one major focus of the Center of Continuing Education at Scarritt College in Nashville from its beginning in 1972. Women have had a major role in planning and carrying out the programs. A new Center of Women's Studies will increase further its resources in this area.

Resources for the long-term leave and the sabbatical. Universities and seminaries are the primary resources for the long-term leave and one-year sabbatical. If you know the study which you want to pursue, the problem is simplified. It then is a matter of finding the school or cluster of schools where good resources in that subject are available. Supplementary resources, however, may affect your choices considerably. My own predilection is for a sabbatical in a large urban center with its multiplicity of educational institutions and cultural opportunities—a predilection confirmed by my own recent experience with a four-month leave in the greater Boston area.

Your choice will be affected by how you decide to draw upon the resources available. If you decide to work on a graduate degree, more choices will be made for you. Many persons, however, organize their own program, either taking classes for credit,

[17] Compiled by Sarah Bentley (Doely) and published by Thesis Educational Resources. The study packet is available from United Methodist Women, the guided study from Perkins School of Theology.

or auditing them, building a program designed to meet one or two central needs, and others also.

Directors of continuing education in some seminaries are prepared to help you plan a long-term leave or sabbatical program. They know not only the educational resources of their school but other educational and cultural resources as well. They can usually help find housing.

Another sabbatical resource is only now beginning to be used—a congregation where ministry is effectively practiced. This is one expression of a trend gaining momentum—to look to one's own professional colleagues, as well as laity, as resources for education. Recently, a minister whom I know was employed by a congregation during his six-month leave, not only to observe it, but also to test some experimental programs of group work in it. In another case a minister and his wife visited and studied on site a carefully selected group of churches where renewal was believed to be taking place. In some urban areas such churches and educational institutions could be combined as resources.

LOCATING PROGRAM RESOURCES

Building your own program of continuing education requires much more specific information about educational programs than this chapter provides: Do they exist? where? when? cost? educational method? and so on. Many of us have been motivated to get underway in continuing education only to be frustrated because we lacked such specifics. Having surveyed the categories of program resources available, let me now point you to the channels through which you can get specific information. Here are some suggested lines of contact (addresses may be found in Appendix I).

1) The continuing education office of your denomination. (Most major denominations now have them.) A call or letter can provide specific information or tell you where to find it.

If your denomination does not have such an office, one of the others will be glad to serve you.

2) The Society for Advancement of Continuing Education for Ministry (SACEM) provides an information service for its members and others. This office keeps the most comprehensive file of continuing education programs and resources available.

At present SACEM provides two printed information resources: an annual selective listing of programs organized in five regional guides; a newsletter for members which occasionally lists and briefly describes new program opportunities as well as printed information concerning continuing education.

3) National offices of specialized agency networks, such as CPE, NTL, or Action-Training Coalition can provide lists of centers and/or certified trainers in your region.

4) Local judicatories, whether annual conference, synod, state convention, or some other form, may have a committee on continuing education whose chairman and other members have a considerable amount of program information and know where it may be secured.

5) Interdenominational agencies. Several states and regions now have interdenominational groups whose primary purpose is to provide information on program resources and to help individuals and groups take advantage of them. Some of these are related to state councils of churches; some are independent; some related to state university extension programs. Some are listed in the SACEM resource guides. If one for your state or region is not listed, the SACEM office can tell you whether one exists.

6) Seminaries and other schools. Many seminary continuing education directors are widely knowledgeable of resources, can provide information, and are willing to counsel with you. Increasingly seminaries see continuing education counsel as a major service for alumni and others. You cannot automatically

assume that a seminary is prepared for this service, but it may well be.

Universities can tell you what they have available. The best office for the initial inquiry concerning special programs for church professionals will be the extension center (either agricultural or general; land grant colleges may have both; others only a general extension center, sometimes called a continuing education division). The number of ordained clergy on the staffs of university extension centers is high.

The fact is that an amazing, loosely formed network of persons has developed in the last decade who are equipped to provide information. An inquiry to any one of the above sources can probably put you in touch with the information you need. *That* you inquire is more important than *where* you inquire.

SUPPORT RESOURCES

A basic premise of this book is that final responsibility for designing and carrying out a continuing education plan belongs to each of us individually. To plan our own continuing education program and carry it out is a manageable task, but most of us need assistance along the way. Fortunately support resources for our continuing education are available and—for the near future, at least—will grow. Three kinds are needed by most of us at certain periods: provision of time; money; counsel in planning.

Time. No one can offer you the time for continuing education on a silver platter. Others can help, but finally the responsibility is yours.

Effective time management is perhaps the most decisive factor in determining whether you will engage in continuing education or perpetually postpone it. Before noting the resources for provision of time, let us look briefly at time itself as resource.

My own perception of time as resource was sharpened by the

chapter "Know Thy Time" in Peter Drucker's *The Effective Executive,* a book which I heartily recommend. Written primarily for the business executive, it can be readily applied to our professional situation.

> The supply of time is totally inelastic. No matter how high the demand, the supply will not go up. There is no price for it and no marginal utility curve for it. Moreover, time is totally perishable and cannot be stored. Yesterday's time is gone forever and will never come back. Time is, therefore, always in exceedingly short supply.
>
> Time is totally irreplaceable. Within limits we can substitute one resource for another, copper for aluminum, for instance. We can substitute capital for human labor. We can use more knowledge or more brawn. But there is no substitute for time.
>
> Everything requires time. It is the one truly universal condition. All work takes place in time and uses up time. Yet most people take for granted this unique, irreplaceable, and necessary resource. Nothing else, perhaps, distinguishes effective executives as much as their tender loving care of time.[18]

Drucker also points out that much of our time is not our own. Every business executive and professional person has time demands which virtually cannot be changed. Reordered, perhaps, but not fundamentally changed. We also have, however, discretionary time—time which we can order as we will. Drucker recommends that for certain basic tasks we set aside blocks of this discretionary time adjusted to our own attention spans and hold them quite inviolable. The following observation has had telling effect for my own work.

> One of the most accomplished time managers I have ever met was the president of a big bank with whom I worked for two years on top-management structure. I saw him once a month for two years. My appointment was always for an hour and

---

[18] (New York: Harper & Row, 1967), p. 26.

a half. The president was always prepared for the sessions—and I soon learned to do my homework too. There was never more than one item on the agenda. But when I had been in there for an hour and twenty minutes, the president would turn to me and say, "Mr. Drucker, I believe you'd better sum up now and outline what we should do next." And an hour and thirty minutes after I had been ushered into his office, he was at the door shaking my hand and saying good-by.

After this had been going on for about one year, I finally asked him, "Why always an hour and a half?" He answered, "That's easy. I have found out that my attention span is about an hour and a half. If I work on any one topic longer than this, I begin to repeat myself. At the same time, I have learned that nothing of importance can really be tackled in much less time. One does not get to the point where one understands what one is talking about.". . .

Needless to say, this president accomplished more in this one monthly session than many other and equally able executives get done in a month of meetings.[19]

The daily diet of continuing education requires planned blocks of discretionary time. Effective and busy pastors and other professionals in all sizes and kinds of church organizations find and use them. In the final analysis, of course, decision depends on the degree to which you believe that continued learning is a requisite of competence in a responsible ministry. The ability to decide, furthermore, is not unrelated to emotional health.

Even though the final responsibility for time management rests with us individually, it is still helpful, and often necessary, to have the support of others. If, for instance, a pastor-parish relations or similar committee understands that we view regular study time as essential to competence, they can help interpret that to the congregation.

Support is especially important for the time required for

[19] *Ibid.,* p. 48.

programs away from home. Many congregations now have established policies concerning study leaves for their pastors or other staff. I have talked with many from all sizes of congregations who have said that when the question was raised with the committee or governing board, they found a surprisingly quick positive response. Not long before writing this, I talked to a pastor from an area of the country in which pastors in his denomination have not taken study leaves on any regular basis. He had been invited to participate in a two-month program in which he had strong interest. He believed that it would significantly enhance his ministry and yet was reluctant to ask for that much time away. He said, however, that when he requested the time and interpreted the program's value, he found positive response and unexpected financial help. In other cases, of course, it is an uphill battle. Positive support can be facilitated when we take the congregation into our confidence in planning our continuing education.

Local and church-wide denominational groups have taken action to support time provision for continuing education programs. The United Methodist *Discipline* suggests that the minister be allowed at least one week each year and at least one month during one year of each quadrennium. Many United Presbyterian, USA, presbyteries ask that the congregation write time for continuing education into the pastor's call. Similar actions have been taken by other denominations.

Money. Few of us can completely finance our own continuing education, especially when it requires periods away from home. In fact, my experience leads me to believe that many more ministers and other professionals would be involved in continuing education programs if they had financial help. Money and motivation are not entirely separable.

Beyond our own pocketbooks, five primary sources of financial help are available.[20]

---

[20] A pamphlet which comprehensively lists financial help available to church professionals is available from SACEM.

1) Congregations or other employers. Many churches now include an item for continuing education in their annual budgets. To institute this may require only some interpretation by you. The amount necessary is usually small in comparison to the total church budget.

2) Local judicatories. In The United Methodist Church this is now the most substantial source of support. The majority of annual conferences have grant-in-aid monies available for ministers upon presentation of a sound proposal. Plans for financial support by local judicatories in other denominations is spotty, but present in some cases. Gradually gaining support is a plan whereby a retired minister is employed to fill in for a pastor on a less-than-one-year leave while he or she receives the regular salary.

3) National denominational bodies. The Lutheran Church in America and the United Church of Canada have established national plans to provide general financial support for their ministers' involvement in continuing education programs. In some denominations scholarship funds have been established for special programs. Some of them are available through the offices of continuing education listed in Appendix I; others through program agencies concerned with special areas such as missions.

4) The Parish Ministers Fellowship, Fund for Theological Education.[21] A substantial grant is offered for from six weeks to one year of study for pastors not over forty who have been graduated from seminary between seven and twelve years.

5) Scholarships and fellowships offered by schools and specialized agencies. Some colleges and universities have scholarships available for graduate study in areas relevant to church professionals, e.g., the scholarships for ministers to study adult education at the University of Indiana. Inquiry from individual schools is necessary to unearth these in your own area of interest.

A few seminaries have grants available for short- and long-

[21] Research Park, Building J, 1101 State Road, Princeton, New Jersey 08540.

term study, such as the Merrill Fellows program at Harvard Divinity School and the Masland Fellowships at Union in New York city. The Auburn program at Union makes grants to groups of clergy, and sometimes laity, who devise especially creative proposals for learning together in the field. Some specialized continuing education agencies have grants available. For both these and seminaries, letters of inquiry will obtain the information.

Counsel in planning. Neither this book nor any other printed material can provide all the help needed to plan an individual's continuing education program. Personal counsel is essential, especially after one has passed the beginning steps. In chapter 4 I mentioned Career Development Centers as a resource for helping assess needs. That is one of the most important assists we can have in planning. Many centers are also prepared to help one set career and learning goals and map out continuing education programs to meet them.

Numerous persons and agencies are available for counsel:

1) Seminary directors of continuing education, many of whom have training and experience which equip them to help reflect on personal-professional needs. Many also have broad knowledge of program resources beyond their own schools.

2) Respected professional colleagues. The "tribe" is growing of those who have had extensive involvement in continuing education and have much helpful expeience to share about their own planning as well as resources. The colleague group, which we noticed earlier, is being used by many as a sounding board and source of information for planning.

3) National denominational offices responsible for continuing education. Many of the staff are competent in helping ministers assess needs, but such a process has severe limitations when remote. The primary counsel for planning from these offices is in identification of resources.

4) Staff members of Career Development Centers and similar agencies. Many individual career assessments include counsel

in continuing education, as in the case of Elliot described in chapter 4. Increasingly, staff members are meeting with groups in the field as consultants in career evaluation and continuing education planning.

5) A local congregation or other group. This is one of the most available resources, yet the one most often missed. The members of one's congregation (or other employing group) do not have complete information about program and other resources, but they do have two data which are crucial: knowledge of their own needs and knowledge of their professional leader arising from daily association. Any continuing education plan which does not take these data into account is impoverished if not perverse.

Chapter VI

CAREER DEVELOPMENT AND CONTINUING EDUCATION

Career and continuing education are vitally linked. The development of our careers has more bearing on our continuing education than any other single factor. Thus, career goals, the stages through which a career passes, and growth as a professional person cannot be disregarded in sound planning for continuing education.

By the same token, continuing education is a powerful career determinant. Growing competence is necessary to reach responsible career goals. Continuing education is its major ingredient. "Young men [and women] who perceive competence as a major dimension of ministry thus enter the occupation with a tremendous built-in developmental force. Recruitment programs, seminaries and continuing education programs which deliberately encourage this drive toward excellence . . . are enhancing their career development." [1] This chapter is intended as a tool which will enable you to examine your own career development and to assess its implications for your continuing education.

CAREER DEVELOPMENT

The first task is to clarify what we mean by "career development." It is widely used, but not always understood. In

[1] Edgar W. Mills, "The Minister's Career Development," *Consultation on Continuing Education*, p. 44.

1973 I attended a series of meetings involving more than six hundred persons who are responsible for ministry concerns in The United Methodist Church. No term was more frequently used than "career development." I soon recognized, however, that the term was being used in a wide variety of ways. Occasionally I would ask someone what he or she meant by it, and more often than not the response was indefinite.

No one definition could be proposed which would satisfy everyone, but it will be useful to state a definition which will serve as a working definition here and will, I hope, be useful to you as you work out your own as we proceed.

The key term is "career." To define it takes one a long way toward understanding career development. It is an in word in contemporary speech. "Which do you want, a job or a career?" the radio announcer asks in advertising the services of a placement agency. He knows our answer. We want a career—doesn't everybody? Most of us as professionals in the church know that we are involved in a career—that our working years are somehow joined together in a process. Yet many of us would be hard pressed to say just what it is.

Try this definition on for size: *Career is a way to conceptualize the span of one's working years in terms of its being: a developmental process; affected by personal and social forces; and moving through several definable stages.*

Sometimes, a change of jobs is so pronounced (businessman to minister; advertising executive to craftsman) that we speak of a new career. I prefer to think of such changes as movement from one subcareer to another, reserving "career" for an individual's total working life.

Sometimes, "career" includes the years of educational preparation as well as retirement, especially as the latter becomes a longer, more active period. I prefer here to use the term only for the preretirement working years, especially in reference to the concerns of this chapter.

The idea of a career is relatively new; the fact is not. The cobbler in a medieval village served an apprenticeship; his first week of work in his own shop felt different than the last; at some point he began to contemplate the day when he would finally lay down his tools. In other words, he had a career.

The idea or concept of a career has become widespread only within the last twenty-five years. Within that time a science of career psychology has focused attention on the concept and has examined its dynamics.[2] The study of careers in turn has been informed, and indeed made possible, by the study of adult development. Ego and personality psychologists have turned increasingly to the study of adult development, and their work now points to the fact that we as adults undergo continuing development, perhaps with stages as distinct as those experienced by children and youth. This has heightened the awareness that we progress through stages in our working life. More important, it has provided valuable data for understanding the nature of these stages. But more of that later.

But like "career," "career development" is used in various ways:

1) Movement from one job to another or—rarely now—through only one job in the course of a career. Movement may also be from occupation to occupation.

   This is the simplest usage, but legitimate. Many careers are in fact a nonintentional progress through a series of jobs or occupations until retirement.

2) Advancement in terms of prestige, salary, responsibility. This is a concept of career which can easily be incompatible with ministry. Yet it is one commonly held in our society, and is not necessarily incompatible with responsible ministry.

---

[2] One of the major career psychologists is Dr. Donald E. Super of Columbia University. Dr. Super's book, *The Psychology of Careers* (New York: Harper & Row, 1957), and his many articles have influenced this field widely and have been significant for those studying the career development of church professional leaders.

3) Progress through the several career stages defined by career psychologists.

4) Intentional movement toward career goals.

My own definition of career development is as follows: *Career development is intentional movement toward established but flexible career goals, taking into account the stages through which a career moves and the personal and social dynamics which affect it.*

Career development thus defined does not presuppose any particular job pattern. One career in ministry may progress steadily through a series of pastorates; another, through a variety of jobs within the church; still another from employment by the church to employment outside and then back. But the movement is intentional—the opposite of aimless drifting. Career development, in this sense, is goal-related activity characterized by decisive movement.

One other basic comment is important before moving on: career development is affected by two major forces—the personal and social. On the one hand, it is affected profoundly by the inevitable development of the adult personality, personal physical and emotional health, and by the personal decisions one makes. On the other hand, it is affected by interaction with social forces and groups: the family, the organizations for and within which one works, the culture, peer groups, and the rest. As we proceed, these two major forces will not always be mentioned explicitly, but it can always be assumed that they are present.

CAREER STAGES

Your career, any career, will move through several definable stages. When we have a clear view of these stages we have a valuable tool for intentional career development. This is partly personal testimony. Knowledge of career stages has not solved all of my own career development problems; a tool is just a tool. It has become, however, a tool of growing usefulness. I believe that the same can be true for you.

A career with its several stages will look something like this.[3]

Late Formal Education	The Establishment Stage	Midcareer Stage	Pre-retirement	Retirement
Trial Period	Advancement Period			

This career line is vastly oversimplified. No one, e.g., suddenly steps over a line from one stage to the next; stages merge into each other. Or, someone in mid-career who changes professions may enter a short new trial substage. And so on. Nevertheless, this line represents the way in which many of our careers take shape and move toward termination.

A brief survey of the career stages follows to provide a synoptic view. Following that, each stage is examined in depth.

The *establishment stage* begins the career, continuing until one feels the impact of middle age and the job realities which go along with it.[4] As the term suggests, this is the period when we become established in our work, first through a *trial period* when, in a sense, we try the job on for size, then in an *advance-*

---

[3] This career line is derived in part from an address by Dr. Donald Super at a consultation in 1966. Cf. "Career Development: Life Stages, Developmental Tasks, and Individual Difference," in *The Church and Its Manpower Management*, Ross P. Scherer and Theodore O. Wedel, eds. (New York: National Council of Churches of Christ in the U.S.A., 1966), pp. 65-74. In this address Dr. Super adapted his career development theory to the careers of professionals in ministry. Since then, a growing body of data has accumulated and theory has been projected about the careers of professional church leaders. Much empirical research, however, remains to be done in order to have a foundation for an adequately developed theory.

[4] Super and other career psychologists include two earlier stages: *growth*, when the child lays the foundations for a later career, and *exploration*, when the adolescent clarifies a self-concept and begins to translate it into adult occupational terms. For our purposes it will be more useful to consider a career as beginning after formal schooling at the start of the first full-time job.

ment period when we tend to move ahead rapidly toward career goals.

Somewhere around age forty, we realize that we are no longer young adults and that opportunities for advancement are not limitless—to say the least. We tend to maintain or conserve gains realized earlier. Accordingly, Super and others call this the *maintenance stage.* However another dynamic is also at work. We are likely to feel strong new powers and urges to produce or generate new things. "Maintenance" thus seems inadequate; we often do far more than just maintain the gains of the establishment stage. I have chosen to call it the *mid-career stage,* a neutral term which militates less against the possibilities of new productiveness.[5]

Sometime before retirement, thoughts and feelings about it begin to loom large. At whatever point these become a prominent factor in career activity and decisions, we enter the final formal stage, *preretirement.* Super calls this stage *decline.* To be sure some life powers decline; some things inevitably wind down. Nevertheless, some powers of learning and work can remain strong and even increase. Hence decline seems to me a highly prejudicial term. I much prefer preretirement which again is neutral but describes the predominant dynamics of the period.

Entrance into each career stage is likely to create a crisis. Movement into the establishment stage from schooling creates an early entrance crisis as one gets the feel of full professional practice for the first time. Entrance into mid-career involves the human bio-psychological crisis of middle age as well as of the real or imagined job plateau. Entrance into preretirement involves a crisis centering in a *termination awareness* which may introduce vividly the consciousness of life termination as well as job termination.

In what follows, we will look at each career stage or substage

---

[5] Super himself questions the adequacy of *maintenance* but along different lines.

in terms of: (1) its characteristics; (2) its entrance crisis; (3) its implications for continuing education. Each of you will likely be most interested in the stage in which you now are or through which you have just passed. It may be useful to read about it first. I hope, however, that you will examine each stage. A view of the entire span will increase your understanding of each one.

THE ESTABLISHMENT STAGE

All career stages have their own substages. In this chapter we will examine only the substages of establishment. They are sufficiently distinct, especially in their dynamics, to merit a separate look at each one.

The Trial Period.

1) *Characteristics.* Career development is, in one sense, implementation of a self-concept in the world of work. During adolescence we gradually establish a self-concept. Choosing among the models which we have accumulated, we make hazardous and often stressful choices, gradually constructing a self-image—the person we believe ourselves to be. The self-image usually has an occupational dimension. Some of the models which we try on for size are taken from respected adults who are doctors, lawyers, mechanics, social workers, ministers, etc. Some we like; others do not fit.

During the same years we also realize that we must find our place in the vast and complex world of work. Usually, during college years the matter takes on decisive seriousness. We start to project seriously our self-concepts into the world of work to check out how a given vocation might feel. In other words a trial period begins. Those who are considering a profession or other work requiring graduate education must take some early risks of engaging in trial through education, expensive in both time and money.

If at the end of formal schooling, seminary in our case, we feel that we are on the right track (at least not on an entirely wrong one) we enter our first full-time pastorate, assistantship, director of Christian education, or similar position. Now we are fully into our career, but probably not fully committed to it; we are still in a trial period. Thus in the diagram above, the trial period extends from late formal education (what Super terms the *exploratory stage*) into early years of establishment.

Once into our careers, trial takes on a different quality. As Super puts it, "The young careerist is now playing for real stakes." [6] Now we experience the job as hard reality and must try it on for size, not as anticipated, but as is. It is time to test whether, in fact, our developing self-concept can be fitted to the demands of the profession.

The question must be asked in relation to a particular job in a particular place. We may feel that the first job fits so well that future jobs (and hence the profession itself) will fit. The job, however, may not fit our self-concept; it may in fact produce great stress. The misfit may be so severe that we question seriously the profession itself. Or, more likely, we assume that the job— the particular congregation, the senior minister, or some other factor—is uncharacteristic, and other jobs should be tried before final decisions are formed. This trial period, which may continue for as long as five or six years into the profession, may also involve quite naturally several job changes.

Super and others have pointed out that trial may have one of two basic outcomes: *stabilization* or *floundering*.[7] Stabilization is practically self-defining. We become "located in a career"— at least for the time being. At best, stabilization occurs because one feels that the job fits his or her self-concept, and the choice is made. At worst, it is resigned acquiescence. "The profession

[6] "Career Development," p. 67.

[7] Super treats stabilization as a substage of establishment in some writings (*Psychology of Careers*); in others as a process during establishment ("Career Development"). I find the latter more useful.

doesn't fit me, but what can I do? I've been through seminary; I'm in debt; my family's coming on. How can I possibly change professions now? I'll settle down and endure it." That is stabilization at its painful worst.

Years ago I had occasion to go to a young doctor in a small Oklahoma town. As he treated my minor wound he seemed cumbersome and ill at ease. He appeared to be unhappy yet resigned. Unless I missed the signals this man had stabilized in a profession, but far from positively.

The other alternative is floundering. Strictly speaking, floundering is an aimless movement from one job to another. "There is no sequence or progression, nothing in one job that draws on experience in the preceding job or that leads logically to the next." [8] In that sense it is virtually the opposite of purposeful trial.

Floundering, however, can be the unfortunate outcome of what begins as purposeful trial. "The next job [mirage-like] may be the one that will bring me satisfaction. If this one doesn't fit my self-concept perhaps the next one will." And so some persons move through the early professional career with no real goals, no planned development, not building on experience, only vainly hoping that the next job will be better, until finally they resign themselves to failure.

Until now we have talked of the trial period in terms of job mobility. What happens in terms of the job itself?

The most general process taking place is what we may call *socialization,* i.e., not just trying a job on for size but discovering and adjusting to its demands, then implementing our self-concept in and through it.

Socialization, however, is not a process which begins with a career. It is descriptive of what happens to us from the beginning of life. When for some reason it breaks down, human

---

[8] Super, *Psychology of Careers,* p. 112.

tragedy results. F. W. Allport, a social psychologist, describes it in these words:

> In order to be adapted to civilized society a man must not only be sensitive to the social objects about him; he must also develop permanent habits of response which are in accord with the necessities of group life. Such development may be called the socialization of the individual. It consists of a modification of the original and purely prepotent reflexes through instruction received in the social environment.[9]

Beginning in infancy socialization continues into adulthood. College or university continues one part of our socialization which early schooling began. But it introduces new demands quite uncharacteristic of earlier school days.

When we begin our careers socialization continues, but with a new constellation of demands. Orville Brim lets us feel the impact of those demands:

> In a complex, pluralistic society, such as the United States, many persons and groups compete for effective influence over the behavior of an adult and seek to alter the adult's personality in large or small ways to accommodate their own desires. The differences and conflicts between the objectives of these various persons are manifest in the efforts at adult socialization. The employer, the wife, the child, the advertiser, the physician, the politician—each in his or her own way has an interest in the adult's personality and behavior and seeks to remake it to his own advantage. The fashion industry conflicts with the husband's wishes about his wife's behavior, while the liquor industry competes with the wife in attempting to change her husband's habits. Each group has its own modes of attempted influence, and each has its relative persuasive power. The control over powerful rewards and punishments in the hands of the employers and family members make them especially effective in socialization efforts, while on the

[9] In *Socialization and Society*, p. 35. Cf. Edgar W. Mills in *Ministry in the Seventies*, John E. Biersdorf, ed. (New York: IDOC-NA, 1971), pp. 98-117.

periphery of influence are neighbors, political groups, advertisers, and others.[10]

Super singles out the primary groups in terms of whose demands socialization occurs: those in authority over one; co-workers; family and home; the local community. As he rightly points out, while the young worker is adjusting to family demands, the family unit of which he or she is a part is also adjusting to new demands of community and (in our case) the congregation or other church employer.[11] Thus a double set of dynamics is in interplay.

In addition to the pressures of socialization experienced by men, the young women entering the ministry face a special constellation. The role expectations of the church are much more confused and confusing for her than for the man. She faces resistances to her even being a minister, the nature and intensity of which it is difficult for men to understand. From many of her male colleagues in ministry she experiences hostility and resistance. For some time to come, the impact of the early period in ministry will be greater for women than for men. As we shall see later, this fact has marked effect on the early career crisis of women.

The forces are powerfully present, and when we step into the first full-time professional job we feel their impact. But socialization need not lead to conformity or accommodation. It is interaction of society and self. In the mix is our own will, its values and purposes. We feel society's demands; we also shape society. We adjust to the profession; we also shape the profession. The job affects us; we affect the job. Skill, artistry, and commitment to chosen values are required to strike a right balance between the two. When rightly understood, the socialization of adult life is an exhilarating challenge.

Socialization involves the selection of the roles we will fulfill

[10] "Adult Socialization," *ibid.*, p. 187.
[11] *Pscyhology of Careers*, pp. 115-18.

in relation to the roles expected of us. We leave seminary with a more-or-less defined set of roles influenced by our studies, field experience, previous jobs or professional experience, and by our own self-concept. We then encounter a set of role-expectations held by members of the congregation, perhaps a senior minister or another superior and judicatory officials. In this mix we work out both a definition and a hierarchy of the roles we see ourselves fulfilling in the profession. Usually we integrate these within a dominant or controlling image of ministry.

A recent study by Dr. Warner Heston, Jr. has shown that the group of young pastors studied engaged in this task quite effectively. The group was small, forty-six, but a good cross section. During the early years (approximately six) in the profession, a high percentage of the young pastors established a fairly complex set of defined roles and integrated these into a dominant image. The image most frequently formed was what Dr. Heston calls "pastor-counselor": 57 percent at seminary graduation; 65 percent during the first two years; 70 percent at the time of the study.[12]

Summarizing his findings in relation to this matter, Dr. Heston says that

pastors typically, sought to achieve this kind of effectiveness primarily through their performance of functional roles that in themselves, complemented the desired results: (1) *pastor counselor* in response to individual needs for the kind of maturity that leads to ministry and (2) *organizer-enabler* of the performance of those ministries by their people. They also employed the basic and traditional roles that have always been central to professional ministry—preaching and teaching—but

[12] Warner R. Heston, Jr., "Occupational Role Differentiation in Early Career Development of the Protestant Parish Ministry" (Ph.D. diss., North Carolina State University, 1973), pp. 50-56. At the time of the study the other three most frequently held images were, in order, organizer-facilitator, preacher, educator-scholar.

apparently to support the effective performance of the primary roles.[13]

No matter how well we negotiate the trial period, it will likely involve stress. *Stress in the Ministry* by Mills and Koval, reports a study of 4,908 ministers which asked them to identify major stress periods in their careers and to state the causes. "Forty-two percent of these are reported in the first five years of ministry. For slightly more than one-fourth of the ministers, the first or second year of their ministry was the time of their first major stress period." [14] This does not mean that everyone undergoes stress in the first five years. Neither does it mean that all stress is unhealthy and nonproductive.

A separate but related problem is loneliness. The young pastor and his family have usually established a circle of warm friendships during seminary. Now they are suddenly thrust into a different social environment, sometimes in smaller, rural communities where few couples of similar age live. Friendships usually form, but slowly enough that loneliness is felt.

The more serious loneliness is often professional. Pathetic irony lies in the fact that in the organization ideally characterized by *koinonia,* there is so often mistrust and isolation among its professional leaders. One of the most significant benefits of the Young Pastors Pilot Project, referred to earlier, was that its cluster groups provided a means by which this professional loneliness could be overcome.

To generalize about family life in the trial period is difficult. Some forces pull the family closer together: the initial lack of ready-made friendships; birth of children; the tasks of getting family life underway in a new context. Others create problems: the spouse's awareness of what the job will require—really; lack of money; the time required away from spouse and young children in a period when time together is important. Dr. Heston

[13] *Ibid.* p. 55.
[14] Edgar W. Mills, and John P. Koval, *Stress in the Ministry* (Washington: Ministry Studies Board, 1971), p. 11.

believes that the group of young pastors whom he studied reveal that "the Protestant parish minister who is less than six years out of seminary will have achieved a workable compromise between family and occupational role demands such that the effect is predominantly supportive for him rather than stressful." [15]

One fact about the male minister's wife is now confirmed by several studies: She is a major support to him. (Studies of women clergy are not sufficiently available to support a similar statement about them. I would judge however that the husband is also a major support factor.) This appears to be true all throughout the career, but the trial period is an appropriate place to take note of it since it may be especially important—and influential—then. "Peers and family constitute the bulwark of the Protestant minister's support system. Peer support is probably crucial in most occupations vulnerable to stress, but family support seems especially necessary for clergy. Whatever the liabilities of a married clergy, there can be no doubt that the marital relationship is one of the strongest supports the minister has." [16]

2) *The entrance crisis.* In any one human being the particular mix of the elements we have discussed, and others, go to create the entrance crisis in the trial period. For men, the crisis usually comes in the third to fifth year beyond seminary. For women, it begins almost immediately.

Two major programs and some research confirm this timetable for men. More than a decade ago, The United Presbyterian Church in the U.S.A. initiated a program for its young pastors which is still underway. Its basic premise was that the three-to-five-year period is a deciding or crisis time. The program has confirmed the hypothesis. The United Methodist Young Pastors Pilot Project has also confirmed it.

Why at three to five years beyond school, especially in view

[15] *Ibid.*, p. 78.
[16] *Ibid.*, p. 56.

of the findings that stress begins immediately, the first two years are most often reported as stressful? *Stress* and *crisis,* though often related, are not the same thing. A crisis is always stressful to some degree, but often not severely or nonproductively (sometimes, of course, the stress is severely debilitating). Stress on the other hand, even when severe, may not involve a crisis until it leads into a decision period when basic life issues can go one way or the other.

The years just after seminary may be stressful, but counter forces are at work. During seminary we have usually built up a powerful head of steam: ideas, skills, models ready to be tried. Out ahead is the lure and excitement of a long career which may lead to whatever career goals we have established. We thus accommodate to the stress, viewing it as temporary and provisional.

Several years later, the picture is changed. The head of steam has dissipated. Learnings have been tried and some found unusable. The job has created new learning needs. The reality of the profession's demands has hit hard. We have discovered its joys and hopes, but also its disappointments and despair. Questions begin to appear. "Is it really for me?" "I've had two jobs now, and it isn't what I thought it would be." "I know ministers slightly older who made the break into another profession about now. They are earning more than I am; they appear to be more contented. But are they really?"

For others, the feel of the profession may be far more positive. Substantial evidence indicates that by three to five years into the career many young pastors are satisfied with their jobs and are actively planning for their future. For them the crisis is more along lines of deciding what direction their careers will take. They have stabilized in their careers and are ready to move into the advancement stage. For them, a major decision lies in the style of ministry they will adopt and the further education which will best enable them to attain it.

For the women, the crisis apparently comes much sooner than

for men. Immediately when she begins full-time work after seminary a woman encounters resistances and suspicions which raise questions about whether she has chosen the right profession. No matter how strong her determination, the questions still arise. The possibility of role confusion is high. Most young women in ministry with whom I have talked report that a crisis period begins as soon as the first job and that if a crisis is experienced from the third to fifth or sixth year, it is essentially an extension of the crisis that began in the first.

3) *Continuing education.* The trial period has clear implications for continuing education and closely related processes of career development.

Perhaps the clearest is the need for involvement in a colleague group with others who are also in the trial period. We will say more about the values of the colleague group in chapter 7. Here it suffices to say that no clearer result emerged from the experience of the Young Pastors Pilot Project than that its continuing cluster groups provided an invaluable support-development arena for almost all the participants. Growing numbers of young professionals now leave seminary ready to be involved in colleague groups. Some will find or form a group almost immediately. Women, especially, need a support group soon after seminary. One of the most useful times for involvement of men is during the three-to-five-year crisis period, with a group of colleagues in the same period.

Skill-training is highly relevant in this period. In fact, my conviction grows that only minimal skill-training is appropriate to the basic professional degree. I base this judgment primarily on the mounting evidence that skill-learning occurs best in context. Ministers often fault their seminaries for not having acquainted them adequately with the skills needed to practice the profession.[17] Seminary training may not be nearly as deficient

[17] Dr. Heston's study found a significant number who felt that their seminary education was inadequate in this regard. It also found that those who believed that their seminaries had provided them with adequate "prac-

as it is perceived by graduates. The real problem may lie in the learning readiness of the student. The primary "learning moment" for skill-training comes when one encounters day by day what the job requires. Then, not only is one closely in touch with what the job requires, but can also directly apply the learnings and get immediate feedback. Seminary days may be appropriate for introducing one to the profession (I am convinced, in fact, that seminaries must continue the trend now underway to introduce the realities of the profession early in the seminary degree) and for rudimentary skill-training. The trial period, however, is the time when skill-training can be most productive.

Confronting the reality of the job may also create needs for substantial theological reformulation. Discovering what the church is in its actual sociological existence and what professional leadership requires—or asks for—may necessitate new careful looks at the nature of the church and ministry. One of the most interesting results of Dr. Mills's study of the Young Pastors Pilot Project was that theological reflection increased in the early years out of seminary and that it was closely linked to reflection upon work demands.

The Advancement Period.

If the trial period has resulted in a positive stabilization, the advancement period begins. For many of us, this happens five or six years into our careers. (Again it should be emphasized that boundaries between the stages and periods of our careers are not distinct; they merge into each other.) Advancement continues until the mid-career stage begins.

1) *Characteristics.* During this period we are "on the make" professionally. Energies which have been devoted to determining

---

tical studies and experience" were more likely to have negotiated the trial period successfully, especially in singling out and clarifying the roles required in ministry. "Occupational Role Differentiation," pp. 46-50, 75.

whether we are in the right profession, now are turned toward achieving whatever career goals we have set.

"Advancement" is a tainted word which we church professionals shy away from or have ambivalent feelings about. We have seen those who are consumed with desire for prestige, influence, money, make shambles of a servant calling and create impenetrable masks. That, however, is advancement at its worst.

Advancement at its best is strongly motivated movement toward responsible career goals. Donald Super has said advancement "may consist of better opportunities to play desired roles, more freedom to develop one's own personal style, in other words self actualization." [18] Depending on how we see ourselves and our calling, this may or may not include work in a larger congregation with more salary than in the trial period. It may also include the conscious acquisition of power.[19] Neither of these need be incompatible with the gospel, if rooted in an accurate and developing self-awareness and constrained by the demands of a servant, reconciling ministry.[20]

A primary task, then, is to set responsible career goals, flexible but firm. Who we are as persons, including our strengths, interests, weaknesses; our families' needs; what we feel the gospel requires of us—each is a major consideration in setting goals. This is not to say that we will not have established career goals upon leaving seminary or before. Those, however, may be much more related to getting established in the career than we realize at the time. In any case, once we have stabilized in our careers, it is useful to review goals already set and consider new and substantially different ones.

To establish and develop a professional style is a second major

[18] Super, "Career Development," p. 68.
[19] In part the loneliness of the trial period may be a "power loneliness." In seminary one often has influence upon the life of the school. Once out into the first job, the sense of powerlessness, especially in influencing one's judicatory, may come as a severe shock.
[20] My first inclination was not to use "advancement" as a title for this period. I have retained it because I think it important that we acknowledge the strong aggressive tendencies of this period and harness them responsibly.

task. In the early years, as we have said, we will have differentiated our roles, established a provisional priority for them, and started integrating them into a model. Living out that model is what may be called a style. But a style is dynamic. Throughout our careers, it will change; sometimes the change will be radical enough to say that we have adopted a different style. The advancement period is perhaps the most formative time in development of a professional style.

2) *Continuing education.* We move here directly to implications for continuing education. If the entrance crisis of the trial period has been successfully negotiated, the advancement period is not likely to have its own crisis.

Early in the period, learning which contributes to the formulation of our style and career goals is appropriate. Let me suggest three.

1) A career assessment. Strictly speaking, this is not continuing education. Discovery of strengths and weaknesses and clarification of goals however is an important learning experience and certainly provides significant clues for continuing education planning.

2) Human relations training. To know oneself and relate to others freely and responsibly is the basis of any authentic style. Personal anxiety may be high enough virtually to propel us into some kind of human relations training at this point. Sometimes, however, we trick ourselves into believing that all is well. I know of a number of ministers who early in this period have engaged in CPE programs which have given them a sense of adequacy personally and with others and which have started processes of growth which have continued throughout their careers.

3) Theological studies. By this, I do not mean "returning to the womb" of seminary courses in theology. Study may occur in a number of contexts and should be experientially oriented and in touch with the actual demands of ministry. I realize that the

concept is overworked, but what I mean is that at this point in our careers we learn or relearn to "do theology."

Once we have our bearings, then (unless we have entered the profession late) we have a decade ahead of us to move toward our career goals, modifying them as we go. From the resources available to us we can plan our continuing education activities in terms of enhancing our style and moving toward our goals.

An extended study leave may be an important first step. At one time an extended leave of three to six months would have been exceedingly difficult early in a career. Now, however, denominational policies and support practices make a leave possible, especially if one plans for it purposefully. In an extended leave we can take a major step in the development of skills and knowledge related to our achieving our goals.

THE MID-CAREER STAGE

You feel you have lived long enough to have learned a few things that nobody can learn earlier. That's the reward . . . and also the excitement. I now see things in books, in people, in music that I couldn't see when I was younger. . . . It's a form of ripening that I attribute largely to my present age.[21]

Somewhere in the forties—for most—the middle career period begins. It corresponds closely with the middle period of life. Even if one changes occupations late and is in the entrance or trial phase of a new subcareer, he or she still undergoes the mid-life–mid-career set of experiences. The period ends at whatever point anticipation of retirement becomes a dominant factor in career planning.

[21] Bernice L. Neugarten, "The Awareness of Middle Age," *Middle Age and Aging,* Neugarten, ed. (Chicago: University of Chicago Press, 1968), pp. 93-97; a statement of a man in "the prime of life," one of more than two thousands persons studied in the University of Chicago Committee on Human Development research.

This can be the prime of life when productive powers are at their height. How sad, then, that so many persons in ministry experience it negatively or with only limited satisfaction.

1) *Characteristics.* First, take a look at the summary description distilled from the Human Development Committee's (University of Chicago) study of more than two thousand adults for over a decade.

> In pondering the data on these men and women, we have been impressed with the central importance of what might be called the executive processes of personality in middle age: self-awareness, selectivity, manipulation and control of the environment, mastery, competence, the wide array of cognitive strategies.
>
> We are impressed, too, with reflection as a striking characteristic of the mental life of middle-aged persons: the stocktaking, the heightened introspection, and above all, the structuring and restructuring of experience—that is, the conscious processing of new information in the light of what one has already learned; and turning one's proficiency to the achievement of desired ends.
>
> These people feel that they effectively manipulate their social environments on the basis of prestige and expertise; and that they create many of their own rules and norms. There is a sense of increased control over impulse life. The successful middle-aged person often describes himself as no longer "driven," but as now the "driver"—in short, "in command." [22]

What happens to us, what affects us in mid-career which makes for these characteristics? Two sets of forces bombard us: (1) personal changes, (2) society's attitudes. These, of course, are the two sets of forces which separately and in combination shape our lives from the beginning. However, at certain periods they change character appreciably. That is ap-

[22] *Ibid.,* p. 98.

parently true in mid-life–mid-career. If we labeled the first, P, and the second, S, we could also identify many P-s, S-p, and P-S combinations.

That personal changes occur in the forties can scarcely be denied (although we are inclined to try). Some are outward; some inward. The outward, of course, are more obvious—facial lines, nagging petty ailments, sometimes the first severe illness, and the rest. What others can notice is only part of it. We ourselves sense basic changes in our bodily functions. For women especially, much has been made of the menopause. The menopause, or climacteric, however, is evidently less important than more fundamental changes which underlie it.

What sets both male and female climacterics in motion are changes in the amounts of hormones being secreted by the endocrine glands, particularly those endocrines that govern reproduction. The immensely complicated relationships among hormones are still not wholly clear to us. We do know, however, that they affect not only reproductive capacity, but also energy level, weight, hair growth, skin coloration, skin and muscle tone, body temperature, sleep patterns and general emotional and physical well-being. We also know that the climacteric involves subtle shifts in the hormonal balance that has existed since adolescence among the pituitary gland, the adrenals, and ovaries in women and testes in men. These changes in turn produce a wide spectrum of symptoms, which are, of course, different in men and in women and which also vary widely for individuals within each sex.[23]

These physical changes pull our attention in upon ourselves more than during earlier years. Also, with energy leveling off we are more likely to reassess its use—where we spend what we have.

Human life is of a piece; to separate the physical from nonphysical is difficult. Even so, some of the inward changes at

[23] Barbara Fried, "The Middle-Age Crisis," *McCall's,* March 1967, p. 169.

middle age can be labeled mental or nonphysical. We turn our thoughts in upon ourselves. Reassessment of the self is one of two prevailing themes, says Dr. Neugarten, in the persons studied by the Human Development Committee.[24] Dr. Thomas Brown who is one of the pioneers of the Career Development Centers says of persons in mid-career who have had career assessments, "They were all searching for a new sense of purpose in life and for a way to deal effectively with the *process* of life. None were overly concerned about maintenance of their present life position. They were in search for *meaning,* for a new sense of vocation." [25]

"Middlescence" has rapidly become a popular synonym for middle age. The search for identity and meaning are strikingly similar to adolescence. At middle age we must establish again who we are and why. This is a soul-shaking experience for some; less so for others. But unless it happens, at both periods, we are imperiled for the years ahead.

Our first serious illness is likely to occur in middlescence. Whether it does or not, we will be confronted with the deaths of relatives or close friends. Death thus becomes more immediate than before. I shall have more to say about death's increasing reality in connection with the preretirement period. For now it is enough to say that the experience, combined with our natural bodily changes, is a powerful force pulling us toward inwardness.

How, then, do these personal changes affect our careers? Careers, as we have noted from Super, are to a great extent the implementation of our self-concept in the world of work. When we reexamine our self-identity, we inevitably also reexamine our careers. It is thus natural early in mid-career to examine seriously whether we have chosen the right vocation and if so whether we have set the right career goals for it. A middle-aged dentist was heard to ask with some feeling: "What right did an

[24] *Middle Age and Aging,* p. 93.
[25] Thomas E. Brown, "The Search for Vocation in Middle Life." *Eastern Career Development Newsletter,* Lancaster, Pennsylvania, Vol. I, No. 1, p. 2.

eighteen-year-old boy have to decide that I would be a dentist?"

We come now to the most significant inward factor, "generativity." The term was popularized by Erik Erikson in describing the positive outcome of the crisis at the beginning of middle life. (The negative outcome is stagnation.) This is Erikson's definition:

> Generativity, then, is primarily the concern in establishing and guiding the next generation, although there are individuals who, through misfortune or because of special and genuine gifts in other directions, do not apply this drive to their own offspring. And indeed, the concept of generativity is meant to include such popular synonyms as *productivity* and *creativity,* which, however, cannot replace it.[26]

The readiness to generate new things, to be productive, to create, in middle age is a remarkable fact of which I am profoundly convinced. Personal testimony proves nothing in scientific personality theory. Nevertheless, let me share my experience for what it is worth. Between the age of forty-three and forty-five, some events in my life produced radical new departures for me personally. These, I know, accentuated the other changes which occurred, so I must keep them in perspective. Nevertheless, at about forty-five I felt a new thing in my life; I had not experienced it before in the same way. It was a readiness to produce some things that I could look upon and say, "Large or small, those things are part of my contribution to this world." Two major ingredients constituted this feeling: (1) knowing that I will not live forever, whatever contribution I can make cannot wait for infinite next-weeks; (2) knowledge that I am now able to produce in ways that formerly I was not.

"It's a form of ripening." That's the way it feels. Bernice Neugarten refers to it as a maturing of the "executive processes

---

[26] *Childhood and Society,* 2nd ed. (New York: W. W. Norton and Co., 1963), p. 267.

of the personality." Cognitive psychologists make a good case for the development of the brain's ability to perform ever more complex and non-concrete operations during childhood and adolescence. Is it possible that another stage in the brain's development occurs in middle age actually providing new "computer" facilities not available before? The scientific answer to that will require vastly more study of adults. In the meantime, the studies of adults by the University of Chicago group and many others are establishing that, whatever the psycho-physiological base, in middle age we naturally feel ready and able to produce things we have not before.

How obvious is the relation of this to the drive for competence! The drive which is with us from infancy now takes a new form and experiences a new surge. Again it becomes a motivating force for continuing education and other career development tasks—if we recognize, release, and harness it.

The awareness of middlescence can be grim. Realizing that we are no longer young; the hard realities of the job plateau; the near experience of death—these are gloomy prospects in themselves. But for many, middle age is an exciting period with high hopes, primarily because they recognize and release the drive for generativity.

The second set of forces which bombard us in mid-career come from society. Curiously, American society had made two decisions about the forty-year-old. First, he or she is no longer young—not old, just no longer young. Why forty rather than forty-three or forty-seven is an interesting question. Perhaps it is simply because to think about decades is easiest when making broad generalizations. Whatever the reason, our society seems to have decided it almost as if by vote.

To project the generalization onto society is one thing; to accept the verdict is something else. One of our defenses against death is to pretend eternal youth. Finally to accept the verdict that I am no longer a young adult can be a wrench.

Society's second judgment is that at forty, or thereabouts, men and single women, especially, have advanced in their professions, or businesses, as far as they will go unless they are lucky or exceptionally talented. We may experience the reality of this social myth several years on either side of forty. And social myth is exactly what I believe it to be. In the summer of 1973 I discussed career development in American society with a group of Austrians for most of an afternoon. These were persons with a comprehensive view of that country's culture. They were quite surprised at the idea of a job plateau. They maintained that nothing comparable to a mid-career crisis occurs for men in Austrian society. Men, they said, become more respected in their work and in other aspects of life as they grow older. In many cases, the services of an older professional or businessman come at a premium. My estimate is that the inner youth-age awareness of men in these two societies varies greatly because of the different social attitudes. But, again, research shows that forty is the watermark year in the minds of a vast majority of our population.[27] The job plateau is the widely accepted name for this phenomenon. When the awareness dawns—often by not getting a job one wants—that a person has reached the plateau it is often deeply troubling, especially when mixed with the awareness of being no-longer young.

In addition to these two social judgments, mid-career brings another phenomenon to many married couples, the empty nest. By forty, or soon after, children are ready to leave home or are sufficiently mobile and independent that they are no longer a time drain. If the mother has taken major responsibility for the daily life of the children she now experiences a new freedom. She may seek gainful employment and increase all her activity outside the home.

When this new freedom is combined with an awareness of the new generativity of middle life, a married woman often

[27] For the report of a study concerning both the job plateau and middle age, cf. Bernice L. Neugarten, Joan W. Moore, and John C. Lowe, "Age Norms, Age Constraints and Adult Socialization," in *Middle Age and Aging,* pp. 22 ff.

senses a new exhilaration. Many now either move into gainful employment directly or go back to school and then find a job. The woman's feelings in the empty nest may be quite different than the man's, a fact we shall look at in relation to the mid-career crisis to which we now turn.

2) *The Crisis.* Entrance into mid-career involves a crisis for almost everyone in business, the professions, and many other occupations. The crisis is often considerably different for married women than for single women or for men, as will be noted in this section. Nevertheless, they too experience it.

To read and hear of the mid-career crisis is common these days. Yet I believe that many persons who go through this crisis are convinced that they are alone—at least, that no one else experiences it in the same degree of intensity. If you believe that, you are wrong. The mid-career crisis is a common experience. To acknowledge that is a first step in resolving it productively.

Some persons experience the secondary effects of the crisis rather than the crisis itself, especially if they tend to submerge their feelings or not acknowledge unpleasant realities. If the earlier personal crisis which Erikson describes as "intimacy vs. isolation" [28] has not been positively resolved, the mid-career crisis may show up as dissatisfaction with one's marriage or a strong attraction to a friend of the opposite sex or just a vague desire for an affair. It may show up as boredom with work. An article in *McCall's* several years ago said that "executive fatigue" is reported by physicians to be the number one complaint of middle-aged businessmen. [29] Many ministers at mid-career become bored with their work, sometimes to the point of despair. One can, of course, simply be bored: no job is exciting all the time. But when work is pervaded day after day with a heavy lag, one is likely touching the tip of the crisis iceberg.

[28] *Childhood and Society,* pp. 263-66.
[29] Fried, "The Middle-Age Crisis," p. 173.

Many experience the crisis quite directly, feeling the full force of its impact. For these as well as the others, the first step is to understand what is happening. What, then, is the mid-career crisis all about?

This crisis, like the others, is a basic life decision in response to the new situation with which life confronts us. But the special physical and psychological changes and the changed societal expectations make this one a new ball game.

> The crisis does not stem from any one set of conditions but from the interaction of three factors: the physical, the psychological and the social. In other words, during the tailspin, when a person does not have his emotions quite under control, he must at this moment deal with unmistakable and unwelcome physical evidence that he's getting older and therefore less desirable socially—especially in America where youth is god.[30]

Throughout the advancement period most of us have had career goals which include more salary and prestige than we actually attain. I will readily acknowledge that the career goals of some persons do not include these, and that perhaps the ideal for professionals in ministry should exclude them almost entirely—though I am not completely convinced. But here, we are dealing with what *is* rather than what *ought to be,* and my experience leads me to believe that more salary and prestige are major elements in the career goals of the majority of church professionals during the advancement period. In mid-career few of us escape the realization that to move into a higher salary bracket and to gain more influence because of a larger church or a job with more power is unlikely. The strength of this drive through the advancement period and the premium attached to salary and prestige in American society make this adjustment difficult indeed. Add to that the fundamental adjustment to middle age, and it is little wonder that the crisis of selfhood is as severe as in adolescence—*if not more so.*

[30] *Ibid.,* p. 169.

Here enters generativity. The clouds darken, but a strong ray of light appears. Just when we feel the urge and new powers to produce—to generate—we also are confronted with new limitations of age and the job plateau. How ironic! It is just this clash of powerful negative and positive forces which makes this such a severe life crisis for many persons.

But the same forces which darken the clouds produce a ray of light. Generativity can be actualized. We can discover and use striking new power for many years ahead if we can only revise our self-concept and, concurrently, our career goals. Sadly, some of us fail to do that. Erikson says that the negative outcome of the middle-years crisis is stagnation. Thousands of church professionals stagnate in later years precisely because they have not adjusted their self-concept in ways that release the powers of generativity.

The empty nest has a special bearing on the crisis for married couples. The wife, we have said, may find a heady new freedom and moves increasingly outside the home into new social relationships and, often, gainful employment. This still involves a crisis for her in the sense that she is now making important new choices about her life. Such choices always involve some stress, but the new exhilaration usually far outweighs the stress.

If the husband is experiencing substantial stress in mid-career the empty nest may make it more severe. He finds himself irritated that home is not the same. The children are gone; his wife is away more and more. But more troubling is a failure to appreciate his wife's exuberance. Just when he is experiencing severe limitations, she is finding new freedom. Unless the relationship has been solid, this will create new hostilities and anxieties between them, which in itself compounds the stress caused by the other factors.

Resolving the mid-career crisis positively, involves more than anything else the adoption of new career goals which allow the channeling of the new powers of productiveness. When that happens, the last half of the career can be by far the most satisfying. Not only are we released from the tensions of the advancement drive, but—more important—we experience the profound satisfactions of releasing and using the strong new creative powers which mature only in middle age.

One afternoon in a seminar for ministers in mid-career, I talked privately to a man with whom I felt immediate rapport. He said that the seminar had allowed him to focus and acknowledge his thoughts about leaving the ministry. The evening before he had been able to tell his wife for the first time that he was seriously considering the move. As we talked this man expressed deep disappointment that so often the hopes and plans for programs in his church did not materialize. He would present them to the laity, find initial responsiveness, only to see it quickly lag. He did not say so explicitly, but I sensed disappointment that he had not advanced as far as he had once hoped. As we talked, however, I realized how easy and satisfying it was to talk with this man—how open and sensitive he was. In response to my questions he acknowledged that he enjoyed his personal pastoral contacts and that persons responded to him well. It occurred to me that he had remarkable native pastoral abilities and a high potential for learning to build programs on the basis of genuine lay involvement. Several years later I saw this man again. His whole aspect had changed. Nothing could be more evident than that he had discovered his powers to be productive. His pastoral work was going well, and he was involved in planning a new career development program for his annual conference.

I cite this incident because it is quite unspectacular. This man's new generativity is not world-shaking; what he is contributing will not by itself shift history's course. But to him and those around him it makes all the difference in the world. He has discovered that his power to generate will have beneficial results and be satisfying to him. And without question he is making a lasting contribution to his world as a servant of Jesus Christ.

3) *Continuing education.* Three tasks stand out in continuing education at mid-career: (1) To examine, refine, and, sometimes, rediscover self-identity; (2) to establish new career goals or examine and refine those already held; (3) to acquire skills and knowledge appropriate to the new goals and self-understanding.

To say more about self-identity would be redundant; a further comment about new career goals is appropriate. You may be wondering by this time just what kind of career goals I have in mind. Here are several examples: My own pastor, a man in early mid-career, is an exceptionally effective preacher. His sermons are characterized by openness and honesty. He also has unusual insight into the meaning of Scripture and its bearing on contemporary life. He might at this point in his career decide that to build on this strength will be a highly productive goal through the rest of his ministry. Another friend in mid-career who has had strong interest in social issues, has recently found excitement in Transactional Analysis. He and his wife have decided that it is a human relations technique congenial to them and can be a means of working with couples in their church. To become skilled in TA leadership has become one of his mid-career goals.

Once appropriate goals have been established the next task is to engage in whatever learning programs will best accomplish them. More likely than not they will include major educational enterprises lasting over an extended period.

If a professional in ministry had only one opportunity for an extended study leave during a career, it would probably be most useful at this point. When new career goals are established, a period which allows concerted work on the development of new knowledge and skill is highly appropriate.

As we have seen, an extended study leave also provides a time for personal renewal and self-assessment, both of which are appropriate to mid-career. I am inclined, however, to think that an extended study leave will be most useful after basic personal and professional decisions have been made, i.e., after the mid-career crisis is resolved and new goals established.

The new tensions between husband and wife caused by the empty nest can provide an opportunity to create a new relationship—to "reinvent their marriage." The prospects for deepening relationships around new identities and career goals are bright. Both the problems and the possibilities may well indicate that a husband and wife need to engage in joint learning experiences focused on their relationship, or at least with it very much in mind.

All this is not to say that other miscellaneous learning enterprises will not continue as they have in earlier career periods. Involvement in study groups, personal interests, and particular needs arising from the job will all continue to trigger a variety of continuing education projects.

Mid-career may be a highly appropriate time for a career assessment. This is certainly true if one has difficulty sorting out career goals or if one has the lurking suspicion that a career change is appropriate. We may well come to the day when a career assessment for all professionals in ministry will be standard operating procedure at mid-career—at least as an opportunity, if not an expectation.

One final word about the learning tasks appropriate to mid-career. It has to do with growing self-awareness. As we grow older, it becomes more difficult to acknowledge things about ourselves which involve painful self-discovery. But mid-career may be a last opportunity to break out of life patterns which have shielded us from ourselves and others. It may be a last chance to move into a self-awareness which will allow continued growth throughout the remainder of our lives. To seek help in a process of self-discovery in mid-career can be one of the most crucial learning events of a lifetime. But each of us must be the judge of that.

THE PRERETIREMENT STAGE

At some point before retirement, its anticipation and feelings about it become a strong element in our attitudes toward our careers and the planning for them. At that point, mid-career merges into the preretirement stage. The particular time varies with individuals. Approximately seven to five years before retirement marks the beginning for many. Retirement, of course, ends the period though by no means the career.

1) *Characteristics.* The night before writing this I watched Abraham Beame, Democratic candidate for mayor of New York in the 1973 primary election. A panel on WNET interviewed Beame and other candidates for "the second most important job in America" (or so the moderator said). Mr. Beame was sixty-eight and one of the panelists began immediately to reflect the comments about town concerning his lack of vitality at that age. Mr. Beame quickly replied that his vitality and drive had never been higher. He was the first to come to his office in the morning, he said, and the last to leave at night. He believed that he had all the vigor necessary to do the job (and he convinced me). Then he made a telling point. He said that he had long experience in knowing how New York works. What others would have to spend months learning, he knew already.

Abraham Beame and those like him defy calling preretirement (and retirement itself) a period of decline. If one looks at a cross section of the population Donald Super is probably right in saying:

Aging and decline are characterized by a slowing down of physical and mental processes and by decreased endurance or energy reserve. Impairments of memory also begin to manifest themselves, particularly failure of memory for recent personalities and events. Decline proceeds at different rates and in different abilities in different people. . . . The aging individual usually has some awareness of the fact that some of his capacities are no longer as great as they once were. He recognizes that he is slipping.[31]

Super's statement fits some persons correctly. Their powers are declining, and they know it. But of others almost the opposite is true: some powers decline, but others accelerate so that a "steady-state" is maintained, or their powers actually increase.

This is certainly true of learning. Until approximately twenty-five years ago all studies of adult learning capacities had been cross-sectional. They naturally showed a general decline. But it has always been obvious that the learning powers of some persons increase until they die in old age. This fact and others stimulated a few longitudinal studies of adult learning ability. They showed without question that the adult may indeed continue to increase his or her overall ability to learn until advanced old age. Memory powers inevitably decrease, but the large and complex frames of reference into which new knowledge can be fitted can more than make up for memory decline.

Having said these things, one must hasten to say that, the Abraham Beames notwithstanding, physical and psychic energies do decline for most persons. I would scarcely question Super's assertion that most professionals begin to restrict their activities. Physicians often refuse to accept new patients; CPAs may not seek new clients. Pastors accustomed to serving large churches will often ask for smaller ones. (I dare say that the pastor near retirement often looks back with relaxed and slightly amused wonderment at his early push for advancement.)

Life becomes more introspective. This fact and its roots are perhaps the most important characteristics. The tendency—unless evaded—has begun to be noticeable in mid-career. Now it becomes a dominant characteristic. For one thing, life-maintenance demands more attention. Illness; petty ailments; deci-

---

[31] *Psychology of Careers*, p. 155. For a fascinating discussion of high achievement in old age, cf. Wayne Dennis, "Creative Productivity between Ages 20 and 80 Years," in *Middle Age and Aging*, pp. 106 ff.

sions about where to spend one's increasingly limited energies—these tend to turn one in upon oneself. Occasionally there is a Norman Thomas or an Eleanor Roosevelt who interact forcefully with the world as long as they live. Most of us, however, are inclined as the sixties progress to let the world take care of itself and look after ourselves more.

Introspection is likely to be far more than physical and psychic maintenance. It is also a deepening concern with life's meaning. Death takes on a close reality likely not experienced before in the same way. More of that shortly.

But almost as a counterforce—as generativity is a counterforce to middle age and the job plateau—many persons experience a third wind. It often feels—so I am told by those who experience it—like a desire to make a final significant contribution before the career is officially over or extended on into retirement. Often concurrently with what is seen as a final change in jobs an individual may decide that a new skill or the improvement of one long held will provide new satisfaction. I recall one minister at this stage of his career who had begun a serious study of geriatrics which he believed would help him and his wife prepare for old age as well as increase his pastoral skill with aging persons. The most remarkable thing about him was the gleam of excitement in his voice and eyes as he described the study.

Often the most noticeable characteristic is the cluster of concerns which prepare for retirement itself: finances, residence, part-time employment. Those who work with persons in the preretirement stage or in the act of retirement itself say that these tasks are often somewhat frantic because they have been too long delayed. Others begin the tasks long before retirement.

2) *The crisis.* Preretirement is shorter than establishment and mid-career. It also has a different character in that it is highly anticipatory of retirement itself. The life question becomes again—as in childhood and youth—how long until . . . ?

Thus, the entire period is one of adjustment and crisis,

rather than having its own entrance crisis, i.e., all preretirement is the entrance crisis for retirement itself. Accordingly the deciding to be done is in relation to those characteristics we have described. Will one assess accurately his or her powers? Will one simply coast or begin learning enterprises to prepare for another phase of productiveness? Will one get about the business of preparing for retirement in terms of its basic necessary arrangements? These are the things at issue. Some resolve them positively. Others do not.

But one crisis pervades all these, its resolution affecting their resolution. It is death. Death and retirement are linked in a peculiar way. Both are terminations; one ultimate, the other penultimate. No matter how one rationalizes retirement in terms of possible activities thereafter, it is still looked upon by our culture as the termination of a long road. Who we are—especially as males—is closely identified with our work. Ask a man who he is, and almost always, after his name, he will say a dentist, a lawyer, a farmer, a minister. Work thus defines selfhood. Consequently, no other termination so nearly symbolizes the end of selfhood as does retirement.

The severity of the crisis is determined to a great extent by the degree to which one has come to terms with the crisis of death itself. What, after all, is the "sting of death"? To some extent, I suppose, Tillich and the existentialists are right: death's threat is the threat of nonbeing; closely related is sorrow at relinquishing the things one prizes, including relationships with loved ones. To one schooled in strict fundamentalism, the sting may be a residual fear of eternal punishment. In each of us these are present in some individualized mix. But the severest sting of death, I believe, is none of these. It is the dread of coming to the end of life and knowing that we had this one chance—only this one—and failed. (This is the most crucial point at which God's mercy mitigates the sting. If we believe that, in his mercy, we can face the threat, we can accept our one life.)

Retirement seems like a rehearsal of the denouement. No other termination is so much like death's. At the end of a long span of years which demanded great amounts of energy and time and which represented to such a degree our sense of self-hood, we come to a termination at which we will face the same prospect: I had this one chance and I failed. That prospect more than any other is the fundamental crisis of the preretirement years.

If we have resolved the crisis of death—if it has lost its sting, the crisis of termination of work will be much more easily resolved, and in turn the other crises. If we have not resolved the crisis of death, confronting honestly the prospect of retirement may provide a highly appropriate occasion.

Erik Erikson defines the crisis of the final life stage as "ego integrity vs. despair." He does not relate it to an exact age period, but much that he says about it fits preretirement.

Only in him who in some way has taken care of things and people and has adapted himself to the triumphs and disappointments adherent to being, the originator of others or the generator of products and ideas—only in him may gradually ripen the fruit of these seven stages. I know no better word for it than ego integrity. Lacking a clear definition, I shall point to a few constituents of this state of mind. It is the ego's accrued assurance of its proclivity for order and meaning. It is a post-narcissistic love of the human ego—not of the self—as an experience which conveys some world order and spiritual sense, no matter how dearly paid for. It is the acceptance of one's one and only life cycle as something that had to be and that, by necessity, permitted of no substitutions. . . . Although aware of the relativity of all the various life styles which have given meaning to human striving, the possessor of integrity is ready to defend the dignity of his own life style against all physical and economic threats. For he knows that an individual life is the accidental coincidence of but one life cycle with but one segment of history; and that for him all human integrity stands or falls with the one style of integrity of which he partakes. . . .

The lack or loss of this accrued ego integration is signified by fear of death: the one and only life cycle is not accepted as the ultimate of life. Despair expresses the feeling that the time is now short, too short for the attempt to start another life and to try out alternate roads to integrity. Disgust hides despair, if often only in the form of "a thousand little disgusts" which do not add up to one big remorse.[32]

3) *Continuing education.* Thousands of older adults in the United States enroll each year in adult education courses. Many of them are engaged in pursuits for which they did not have time in earlier years. Some do it for the sheer enjoyment; others to develop a skill or for an introduction to a body of knowledge which they will use in retirement; others to gain proficiency for the years before retirement. I point to this because enrollment in formal courses is often appropriate to preretirement—perhaps more so than in earlier years.

Many choices in continuing education will appropriately be related to preparation for retirement—both its opportunities and its required tasks. Preparation can take the form of enrollment in adult education courses designed for persons not in professional ministry. If one sees oneself as still engaging in part-time professional ministry during retirement, then courses or seminars selected will be primarily related to that. I suspect that we will hear more and more of an extended study leave at the beginning of preretirement to engage in major preparation for it.

Church agencies are beginning to plan preretirement seminars. Their organizers report that some couples enter them eagerly; others are reluctant—I suspect for some of the reasons looked at above. Surely, a good seminar on preretirement would be a useful continuing education venture for couples early in this

---

[32] *Childhood and Society,* pp. 268-69.

period. When well planned, the seminar provides resources for addressing the practical necessities of retirement and also the opportunities and, perhaps most important, provides a supportive and congenial atmosphere in which to examine one's feelings about it.

INTENTIONAL CAREER DEVELOPMENT

A career is like floating a river on a raft. Rudderless, a raft can float a river from its source to its mouth, going where the river goes, moving with its current, only having to push out from the bank now and then. Some careers are like that. Inevitably a career in that sense will "develop." As in one definition at the beginning of this chapter, career development may simply be "movement from one job to another, or through only one job in the course of a career." One simply goes where the job(s) take one resigning one's self to the bishop's appointment or the chance call of a church. There are a few more rapids these days, but the chances are one can simply be carried along. Thousands have been.

Intentional career development is still like being afloat on a river, but now with rudder and oars. Still the river carries one along from beginning to end—sometimes rapidly, sometimes slowly; sometimes turning, sometimes moving ahead. There are still the banks which define the limits of choice. But with rudder and oars one has substantial control over the movement— sometimes moving toward a bank where there are quiet waters, sometimes moving rapidly with the current, negotiating rapids more safely.

The river and its banks represent those forces in our careers over which we have little or no control. And they are present. Aging waits for no one. We have organizational superiors over whose final decisions we may have little or no control—influence perhaps but not control; we have natural abilities and limitations.

But over other factors we do have control if we will exercise it. We cannot reverse the current or eliminate the banks, but the river is wide and we can exercise substantial control over where we go within its banks.

The difference lies in whether we become intentional about our careers. To become intentional is, essentially, to take charge of one's own life, to be inner-directed rather than other-directed. As concerns one's work, it is to choose career goals and work toward them. It is to find out who one is in terms of one's own abilities, interests. It is to enter into discussion with those who have authority to affect where one will work letting them know one's goals and interests. It is to find and cultivate relationships with colleagues, professional and lay, who can provide support and accountability structures and who can help one establish goals and determine how to reach them.

Finally, to be intentional is to build competence. Growing competence is a powerful career determinant. It will not automatically cause anyone to reach a career goal; there are no magic formulas. But without it valid career goals cannot be reached. In fact, to attain a given degree of competence is in itself a significant career goal.

Career development, then, is an intentional process. It establishes goals and, within the limits of reality, moves toward them. In that movement nothing is more determinative than growing competence, and continuing education is its primary nutrient.

Chapter VII

THE COLLEAGUE GROUP

I really don't hate the church
but I'm damn sick and tired of
being lonely.

I would trust any man in our group
in a time of trouble.

For the first time I have discovered
that I could learn from a fellow pastor.

These statements were made by young men who, from eighteen to twenty-four months were members of small colleague groups in the Young Pastors Pilot Project. They are typical feelings of thousands of church professionals who are discovering the small colleague group as a major resource for their personal and professional growth.

Groups vary widely in composition and activity. A group of pastors in Sand Springs, Oklahoma, has met regularly for guided study. Recently they used a guide on worship. Several participants then formed groups with laity in their churches, where for twelve weeks the minister and lay persons worked together as colleagues. A friend returned recently from a year of clinical pastoral education. Within weeks after his appointment to a church in Tennessee he had drawn together a small interdenominational group of fellow ministers who meet regularly for support and work on their ministry. The Christian Educators Fellowship reports that throughout the United States clusters of directors and ministers of Christian education meet regularly for support and to work on their professional skills. Two ministers and eight laypersons met for approximately eighteen months to explore their life-styles and relationships in the light of the gospel. For several months they read and discussed *I'm OK, You're OK*. Distinctions between ordained and nonordained vanished quickly as they shared their experience and problems. For twelve weeks a professor from a seminary, skilled in human relations, met with a group of ministers and their wives as a consultant in their work on communication.

The list could go on indefinitely. The colleague group in its varied forms is and will increasingly become a major resource for continuing growth and development in ministry.

In this chapter I want to state some of the values that I feel it offers; suggest resources available to groups; and finally, offer some clues to their effectiveness.

First, we need to define the colleague group, which is a small group of persons (5 to 15 in number) who live and work relatively close together and meet regularly either for a set period or an indefinite one. But it is not just any group; it is a group whose members come together with the intent of developing a deeper-than-surface relationship as they work together on their common concerns. They are together, not just because they *are* colleagues (in the beginning they may not be), but because they want to *become* colleagues in their approach to ministry. Thus, always in view is not only the content of the project on which they work, but also the quality of group relationships. My choice of "colleague" instead of "peer" as a general designation for such groups is that it expresses this intent.

The makeup of a colleague group can be varied:

(1) a heterogeneous mix of professionals from a single denomination or crossing denominational lines

(2) a more homogeneous group drawn together partly because of specialized responsibilities and concerns; young pastors, women professionals, Christian educators, those near retirement, and so on

(3) staffs of large congregations or group ministry teams

where the need of collegiality is built into the job relationship
(4) a professional with lay members of the congregation—a
group where the professional leader is a fellow teacher-learner-
participant with laity, not one in which the professional has
special teaching or leadership responsibilities
(5) cross-professional groups; health professionals, lawyers,
ministers, working on matters of joint concern.

There are others, but these I see as the major possibilities.

VALUES IN THE COLLEAGUE GROUP

The colleague group has at least five characteristics which
contribute to its value for personal and professional development. These are not absent from other settings, but they do
pertain in some unique ways to colleague groups.

1) *Mutual Support.* Loneliness in one form or another
plagues us. In some places it is because of sheer geographical
isolation. More often it is isolation behind walls of mistrust
and suspicion. Ours is a lonely society anyway, but our profession
seems to attract persons who are not only susceptible to loneliness, but actually pursue it. The young pastor voiced the feelings of thousands of us when he said, "I'm damn tired of being
lonely." The other side of the coin is that when we find a group
of persons we can trust, a positive sense of support emerges
which has value in itself and heightens our ability to increase
our competence and to translate it into effectiveness.

If one result of the Young Pastors Pilot Project stood out
above all others, it was that its cluster groups provided a sense
of support which helped overcome loneliness and opened the
door to developmental work. No setting for continuing education lends itself better to dialogical learning than the colleague
group, especially after its members have developed sufficient
trust to "speak the truth in love" to one another and to listen.
Furthermore, the group becomes, at its best, a significant labora-

tory for learning communication skills, including conflict management.

2) *Accountability.* Church professionals often take courses for credit when they do not intend to apply them to a degree. One reason they give is that credit enrollment holds them accountable for serious study—study which they might not do otherwise, a finding reported especially by sponsors of education programs offered in the field, such as the Academy Program of the School of Theology at Claremont and CHARIS. The fact is that many of us need some kind of external motivation to hold us at a serious study long enough for it to affect our competence. Richard Murray decided that the Perkins School of Theology guided study program should be oriented to groups partially because they would provide an informal accountability system. Experience has confirmed this initial judgment.

As commitment to a colleague group deepens, so does a sense of responsibility to it. Concomitantly, one is likely to feel more personally responsible to carry through the learning projects to which we and the group are committed.

When a group functions at its best, the accountability carries outside the group; participants sense that they are accountable to it, not only for what goes on within the group, but also for growth in competent ministry generally.

3) *Accessibility.* From the beginning of the continuing education movement, Dr. Connolly Gamble has stoutly maintained that one criterion by which any resource must be judged is its accessibility. Time has proven him right. If we are to engage seriously in continuing education, we must feel that resources for learning are easily accessible. In a colleague group they are. Partially because of that, it provides an entry point for many persons who otherwise would not begin a systematic continuing program of learning. But a colleague group is not just an entry point. Throughout any individual's continuing education, it provides an accessible resource of great value.

4) *Immediacy.* The colleague group brings the practice of

143

and learning for ministry into close contact. One of the major contributions of the Action-Training Centers and Clinical Pastoral Education has been their development of action-reflection training. They have done it in different settings and by somewhat different methods, but common to both is the idea that reflection on one's work is an effective means of learning and that the scene of the reflection and the scene of the action must be close enough that one can move between them readily. A colleague group will not necessarily cause this to happen. Physical proximity does not necessarily overcome great psychological distance.

A colleague group at its worst can be a devastatingly effective escape mechanism from the grim realities of the job. That it can be misused, however, does not minimize its potential. Especially if a group learns to use a case-study method, it can provide an apt setting to "learn the practice of the profession from the practice of it."

RESOURCES

The primary resource of the colleague group is its own members. It underlies all the others. If the members are not willing to offer themselves and to accept that offer from others, every other resource becomes a gimmick of little importance. But to share personal and professional experience with colleagues and to learn from their experience is foreign to our usual style of operation. Our conditioning in school has taught us that we really learn from a teacher or specialist—not from one another —so we need to be reminded again and again that we can learn from a colleague, until finally at some crucial life moment we experience it. Then we will not have to be reminded again.

This is a day of highly effective techniques (and not a few silly ones) in group process. So effective have they been that we are likely to think that people cannot open their lives and experience to one another without them. I do not believe that.

If a group coming together will agree: (1) that for this period each person will be free to express the true self to the degree that he or she desires, (2) that no one will be expected to reveal that which he or she does not want to reveal, the results can be remarkable. There will, of course, be obstacles; openness and trust are never built easily. If a group has a consultant available or its members are skilled in the techniques of group formation, then they should by all means be used when appropriate. My point is, that if they are not present, a group can still develop openness and trust. I have seen it happen too many times to believe otherwise.

Here are several resources:

1. *Prepared case studies.* In 1971 I audited a course at the Harvard Graduate School of Business. There was no text, only a set of case studies of large companies with formal planning systems (the subject of the course). In each study the company faced a problem representative of those the students might face later. The case would describe the company and the history which had brought it to a crucial decision. The class would then be asked, in effect: "What would you have done? Put yourself in the position of the decision-makers and use your knowledge and imagination to address the problem." At the end of the period another case was often distributed describing what had actually been done and the consequences. The students compared it to their own decisions, and then examined the appropriateness of the decision the company had made. This brief excursion into the world of graduate business education vividly demonstrated to me the productiveness of the case-study method when well used.

Case studies appropriate to our work are now readily available, and more are being prepared all the time. *The Christian Ministry* as of this writing is publishing two in each issue. *The Journal of the Academy of Parish Clergy* carries them as well. A sample case study is printed in the Appendix II of this book. The Case Method Project at Lancaster Theological

Seminary is one of the agencies from which case studies are available.[1]

2. *Methods for preparing case studies.* The most effective case studies which a group can use are those written by its members reflecting their own work experience. They have a reality factor impossible in the prepared case.

Clinical pastoral education has long since demonstrated that a disciplined case method can introduce work experience into a group far better than informal reporting. That will also be true for your colleague group. You cannot assume that the realities of the job will be effectively brought to the group by casual reporting. Simple case-study procedures are now available which suggest methods of preparation and discussion.[2]

3. *Self-appraisal intruments.* Planned self-appraisal or, if you like, performance evaluation is an activity well suited to a colleague group. When openness and trust have developed there is an atmosphere in which members can help one another assess their competence in ministry and steps needed to increase it.

The Christian Ministry for January, 1973, focused almost entirely on "measuring ministries." In one article, Loren Mead suggests a process for evaluating one's ministry which I have modified slightly for use in a colleague group.

A. The individual to be evaluated chooses someone he or she trusts (in or outside of the group) as a personal consultant during the evaluation. The person is chosen with a view to his or her ability to provide support and intellectual balance.

B. The individual chooses three other group members who will help evaluate his or her ministry. He or she chooses one lay person and asks an official church body (such as a

[1] For information, write Case Study Project, Lancaster Theological Seminary, Lancaster, Pennsylvania 17603.

[2] Cf. James D. Glasse, *Putting It Together in the Parish* (Nashville: Abingdon Press, 1973), pp. 84-105.

pastor-parish relations committee) to choose another, and they together choose a third.

C. Using an agreed-upon statement of the competencies required for ministry (cf. the list of competencies on pp. 41-43), the individual, the three colleague-group members, and the lay persons each makes an evaluation. The individual will also prepare a statement of areas in which he or she wants to increase effectiveness and ways envisioned for doing so with definite statement of proposed steps.

D. The consultant reviews all evaluations and the individual's statement, then discusses them with the one being evaluated.

E. The individual discusses the results with the colleague group using data which he or she and the consultant have agreed should be presented to the group. The discussion at this point would center on the steps planned to increase competence.

F. The individual discusses the results and plans with the colleague group and with a representative group from his or her congregation for ways to increase competence.[3]

4. *Guided study resources.* The guided study resources described in chapter 4 are, in large part, designed for group use. Now more than formerly, the loaned material contains cassette tapes and other guidance materials especially for group activities. For example, the guide, *Women: Perspectives on a Movement,* contains cassette tapes for group consciousness-raising exercises.

For a colleague group never to do more than engage in study programs is regrettable. Nevertheless, group study is a well-suited resource and is often a door-opener to dealing with immediate personal professional concerns of group members.

5. *Electronic communication.* Telephone communication was

[3] "Evaluation? Who Needs That?" pp. 2-4. Mead's suggested procedure is based on an evaluation prepared by the Association of Religion and Applied Behavioral Science in certifying its members for professional practice.

described in chapter 4 also. My conviction is that the next three years will begin to see telephonic networks established in which colleague groups are tied into a central resourcing system. These telephonic networks already exist and are waiting to be used by church groups. They could provide general programming which groups could plug into from time to time. Better still, a network could provide a ready channel for colleague groups to request telephone sessions with accessible persons about a particular need and to request other resources: consultants, study guides, cassette tapes, and similar resources, which the network center could either supply or broker.

Now, prior to the development of such networks, any group can use speakerphone equipment to talk with specialists anywhere in the United States at a relatively small cost per individual.

Closed circuit and educational television is still another delivery system only now beginning to be used, sometimes in conjunction with telephone communication.

6. *Consultants and specialists from seminaries and other agencies.* Seminaries are planning fewer on-campus programs in continuing education and offering more resources for groups in the field. This usually takes the form of seminars and courses for larger groups, but help is also available for small groups. The resources of the Auburn Program at Union and the Hartford Seminary Foundation were referred to in chapter 4. For the Northeast these agencies are providing significant resources for colleague groups of all kinds. Some United Methodist seminaries are committed to provide specialists for these study groups using the New Dimensions guided study program. Several seminaries are linked with Perkins in its guided study program, which also provides for a specialist at the close of a group study.

Persons with group-consultant skills are frequently employed by local church judicatories and national agencies. They are also widely dispersed as institutional chaplains, some of whom have strong interest and job freedom to consult with church professional groups. Here and there, state university extension services have personnel available, as do seminaries. Many times groups assume that no one is available, when only a little initiative would find someone equipped to work with them.

SUGGESTIONS FOR EFFECTIVENESS

No simple list of ingredients and no recipe for the effectiveness of a colleague group exist. Some groups are doomed to ineffectiveness from the day they begin. In others, the mix of persons or the strongly felt needs practically insure that they will succeed. But many lie somewhere in between and often founder for want of a few simple suggestions.

1. The two principal processes in an effective group are group-formation and developmental tasks. When either is neglected or becomes overly dominant, effectiveness will be impaired.

Group formation is the developing collegiality which will both hold the group together and undergird its developmental work. When the group is weak, developmental work is sometimes possible but is not as effective.

2. Trust-building and commitment to an agreed purpose are two primary processes in group-formation.

Trust-building depends greatly upon the member's willingness to be open to and to care for other members. Openness requires honesty about feelings toward others. The group must accept the possibility of conflict and find ways to handle it. If no conflict occurs, trust will likely not build. On the other hand, conflict not well handled can impede group formation or destroy the group.

At or very near its beginning, the group should work out a clear contract as to its purpose (Is it a study group? a general support-professional development group? Is its primary purpose to work on human relations?), the length of its life, and its frequency of meeting.

3. It may be useful to charge someone with special responsibility for group maintenance.

A group may need to have one of its members on the alert to the keeping of the contract and authorized to call failure to the group's attention. This, in most cases, should be a rotating responsibility. The same individual might be the leader of regular or occasional debriefings.

4. A crisis in the life of one of the members may dominate the group's attention overly long and can cause a lessening of the group's interest.

Everyone must feel that with relative frequency his or her own concerns can be worked on by the group. If, because of a crisis or any other reason, one member's concerns dominate the group too long, the group may want to help that member find outside assistance.

5. A balance should be maintained between group formation and developmental work.

In the beginning, group-formation will likely require a larger percentage of concern than later. If trust-building and commitment questions continue to predominate, there may be a lurking problem which the group has not faced. Developmental tasks which the group adopts—guided study, case studies, evaluation, and the like should still allow time for introduction of special personal concerns which members need to introduce. In the long run, unless group members feel that they are doing effective work on their development in ministry, their interest will lag unless the needs for a support group are so strong that that in itself keeps them involved. That itself might be the subject for serious group work.

6. A group will be most effective when it explores continually the various resources available for its work.[4]

___

[4] The suggestions above reflect findings from the cluster groups in the Young Pastors Pilot Project. (*Peer Groups and Professional Develop-*

POSTSCRIPT *(just to keep the record straight)*

Colleague groups are developing so rapidly and demonstrating their effectiveness so well that already there are those who would say—or at least imply—they are the only valid setting for continuing education. In this chapter I have tried to indicate my belief that the colleague group is a significant setting for continuing education. But the colleague group involves neither the cross-fertilization nor the intensive-extensive involvement with a specialist or expert which a good residential program affords. One of the colleague group's greatest dangers, in fact, is that it will become ingrown and provincial—an in-group which thinks that everything outside itself is of little use.

I would also make a case for solitary learning. Sometimes you and I have unique learning needs, but we cannot go away to a program (or none is available)—needs in which a colleague group has little interest. Furthermore, I believe that the human mind is both capable of and requires periods of solitary reading, thought, and reflection as nourishment for its growth.

Allen Tough's recently published study, *The Adult's Learning Projects,* may well be a landmark study in adult education. The adults studied had engaged in self-initiated learning projects the median of which was eight per year (some undertaking as many as fifteen or twenty), requiring an average of seven hundred hours. Two facts are of special interest here: (1) They were, for the most part, *individually* initiated; (2) though the individuals often sought help, "two-thirds of all the projects were planned by the learner himself. All but three of the interviewees conducted at least one self-planned project." [5]

And here is the joker for the single-minded educational dogmatist. The question was asked:

---

ment [Nashville: United Methodist Board of Higher Education and Ministry, 1973], cf. especially, pp. 71 ff.) The data gathered during the evaluation study of the project is a valuable fund of information concerning what helped and impeded the life and work of the groups.

[5] (Toronto: Ontario Institute for Studies in Education, 1973), p. 85.

Please think for a moment about how much knowledge, information and understanding you gained as a result of this one learning project—or think how much your skills and habits improved—or how much your attitudes or sensitivity changed. Again, contrary to what we would have expected, the amount of change or learning in a group is less than in a self-planned project.[6]

Now and then one hears the outright statement or the implication that one can learn almost nothing by himself. How ridiculous! The study by Tough is not only a good corrective to such nonsense, but also a balance to the advocacy of colleague groups in this chapter. There are, after all, many ways to learn and many settings for the enterprise.

When all this has been said, I would still maintain that the colleague group is the richest resource for continuing education for ministry today. It will become even richer.

[6] *Ibid.*, p. 90.

Chapter VIII

CLERGY AND LAITY IN CONTINUING EDUCATION

The relationship between clergy and laity is one of the most important matters to consider in planning one's continuing education. Although this chapter focuses on clergy-lay relationships, most of its ideas apply equally to relationships between lay church professionals and other laity with whom they work. If continuing education were only for self-aggrandizement, there would be less need for concern about the laity. But that is not the case. Continuing education does have intrinsic personal values, but finally it is for the sake of the whole church and its ministry in the world.

THE WIDENING GULF

Unhappily, the gulf between clergy and laity is wide and growing wider. Sometimes the result is conflict; sometimes the laity simply only go their own way either disregarding or disdaining the clergy. In either case communication breaks down. That one can find bright exceptions only highlights the darkness of the total scene.

Conflict between clergy and laity is, in part, rooted in a broader conflict in the church (sometimes producing as much conflict among clergy and among laity as between them), which in turn is part of the conflict in society. This is what Jeffrey Hadden found in the late 1960s[1] and, while the scene has

[1] *The Gathering Storm in the Churches.*

shifted in the 1970s, American society is still experiencing a massive taking-sides, which may be without precedent in our culture. Clergy and laity often find themselves on different sides of sensitive issues and the gulf widens.

The gulf is also widened by the fact that some laity have jobs which involve them in our society's complexities to such a degree that the simplistic preachments of many clergy have nothing to say to them. These are the lay persons who usually go their separate ways, paying little attention to the clergy, though sometimes wistfully retaining membership in the church.

The most basic cause of the gulf may be something less dramatic but more pervasive than either of these—namely, conflicting role expectations. We as church professionals have one set of expectations of ourselves; the laity often have another.

Studies confirm this discrepancy. Between 1964 and 1970, a special commission of The United Presbyterian Church in the U.S.A. studied that denomination's approach to continuing education for ministry. It was central to the study to find out how laity and clergy viewed the latter's job. The study clearly revealed that lay persons saw the clergy's role primarily as one of institutional maintenance and pastoral service to the congregation. The clergy saw it as that, plus the task of equipping the laity for their own ministry and mission in the world. The report summarizes the laity's view as follows:

> It is apparent that these active lay leaders want their pastoral ministers primarily for themselves. They want them to keep close to the congregation and to them personally. They say this despite the fact that the great majority of them do not turn readily to the minister for help in times of deep personal crisis. Perhaps it is for this reason that they regard the distance or gap that they see existing between themselves and the minister as one of the primary problems to be overcome. . . . The point of view that seems to prevail throughout the responses from these laymen is one that seeks to protect, secure and defend against attack from without that which is most

immediately perceived as valuable: in this case, the local congregation itself. This point of view might be described as a defensive strategy, but it is important to our understanding of it that we recognize that it is a perfectly legitimate stance and one that is by no means unknown or unpopular in the life of institutions.[2]

A study of women employed by the church reported in 1972 found role discrepancy to be the most frequent source of dissatisfaction. Forty-one percent of one group and 36 percent of another "felt their jobs being 'unclear to others'" constituted a major source of dissatisfaction.[3]

If the ultimate purpose of continuing education is to equip the whole church for its life and mission in the world, it ought to help close the gap, whatever its causes. Instead, it often serves to widen it. Sometimes just the fact that the pastor has "gone off someplace again" is an irritant. But the causes are more basic. For one thing we tend to select continuing education programs consistent with our own role expectations. If these differ from those of our laity, continuing education only prepares us to do better what they do not expect of us.

Religious language is often a cause for misunderstanding. As church professionals we must of necessity use religious language in communicating with the laity. Using religious language skillfully in order that the Word-event of Christ may become real in us and in others is central to our task.

But religious language can be a bag of silver balls which we enjoy juggling in front of a congregation or in pseudo-dialogue. When that happens we are soon recognized as fakes, especially

[2] *The Blue Book: Part III,* Report to the 181st General Assembly (1969) of The United Presbyterian Church in the U.S.A., pp. 62-63. Cf. Donald P. Smith, *Clergy in the Cross Fire* (Philadelphia: Westminster Press, 1973), for a helpful discussion of role conflicts and ambiguities confronted by the church professional, and suggestions for dealing with them effectively.

[3] Elizabeth Anne Waldrep, "How Satisfied Are Women Professionals in the Church?" *Professionally Yours* (Publication of the Christian Educators Fellowship, The United Methodist Church, Summer, 1973), pp. 4-5.

by the young. But even when we have sincerely appropriated the langauge and are committed to it, communication may still fail because many laity have not the slightest idea what we are talking about or hold such different meanings that we communicate exactly the opposite of what we intend. This sometimes reflects the vast biblical and theological illiteracy of contemporary laity. (But that is no excuse, since one of our major tasks is to help them become literate in the faith.) More often it reflects our own illiteracy and inability to translate religious language, which we do know, into terms which the lay person understands and can appropriate.[4]

Continuing education can make matters worse. We go to a seminar or read a book which either reminds us of the old esoteric language or introduces us to sparkling new terms with little or no attempt to help us appropriate meanings or increase communication skills. The result: the laity see our continuing eduation as harmful to them. Too often they are right!

We could continue to analyze the problem. It is more important, however, to examine how continuing education can help narrow or close the gulf.

TO NARROW THE GULF

Concern to narrow the gulf and to enable continuing education to enhance the ministry of the whole church has stimulated a growing debate about the participation of clergy and laity together in continuing education programs. Some maintain that church professionals should usually engage in continuing education programs without laity present. It makes little more sense, they say, for lay persons to be present than for the doctor to have patients present, or the lawyer, clients, in their continuing education. An increasing number, however, argue that almost no authentic continuing education for the clergy is valid

---

[4] In emphasizing our failure as professionals I do not intend to say that laity do not often have a great deal to teach us about the meanings of religious language.

unless the laity are involved. The crisis is so severe, they say, and professionals and laity so closely bound together in ministry that it creates a false situation to separate them in continuing education.

This debate is useful in focusing attention on the problem and making visible some of the central issues, but it takes the wrong starting point. The place to begin is with the relation of clergy and laity in the church's ministry. One can then ask what that relationship requires for their continued learning. (In this section, for purposes of simplicity I continue to speak exclusively of clergy. The discussion, however, applies equally to lay professional leaders in almost every case.)

The starting point, the foundation, is that ministry has been entrusted by God to the Whole People—the *laos*. As the Plan of Union adopted by the Consultation on Church Union in 1970 says,

> The ministry of the church is one. The ministries of the ordained and the unordained are aspects of this one ministry. Lay persons and the ordained share the same basic vocation to become free and responsible members of the new human community. When God calls and the church ordains some persons for representative ministries as presbyters, bishops, or deacons, both those so called and ordained and those not ordained have responsibility for the ministry as a part of the whole people of God.[5]

Within this one ministry, the clergy and the laity have distinguishable ministries, which nevertheless overlap in large areas. Their ministries are represented in the chart on page 158.

The overlapping area of common ministry (a) includes many joint functions: teaching, bearing one another's burdens, proclamation of the gospel, liberation of the oppressed—these and many more. At the same time each has a unique ministry. The lay person (b) has a ministry in the world which is largely

[5] *A Plan of Union for the Church of Christ Uniting* (Princeton, N.J.: Consultation on Church Union, 1970), p. 38.

Ministries appropriate to laity		
	Ministries appropriate to clergy	
Ministries appropriate only to laity	Ministries appropriate to clergy and laity together	Ministries appropriate only to clergy
b.	a.	c.
MINISTRY	OF THE WHOLE	PEOPLE

closed to the ordained simply because the laity are present there in a way which the clergy are not. The lay person is the one, for example, who genuinely has access to the world of work outside the church and thus has a unique ministry there. Furthermore, laity can minister to one another in the gathered church in ways closed to the clergy. In these days, e.g., the word of a lay person on social issues is often far more credible to other laity than the word of the clergy. Reuel Howe puts it well:

> Clergy do not live where living encounters of the gospel with the secular world are possible. The dialogue between the world and the gospel is the responsibility of the laity whose living is in the complexities and pressures of the secular world.
>
> Again, clergy cannot make Christian interpretations of life or living interpretations of the gospel for the laity. The laity have to make their own, out of their own meanings and in their own terms, and in this process clergy are only the informers, the guides, and, if you will the mid-wives of the process.[6]

[6] "The Continuing Education Needs of the Church's Ministry," *Consultation on Continuing Education* (Consultation proceedings), Ralph E. Peterson, ed. (New York: National Council of Churches of Christ in the U.S.A., Department of Ministry, 1964), p. 68.

The clergy also have ministries which are uniquely theirs (c). Traditionally, leadership in the sacramental role has been reserved by the church for the ordained. The nature of the job also allows time to prepare for proclamation of the gospel and teaching. Most churches also give the ordained by rule or custom a primary role in the ministry of order, or administration. These and other ministries are given to the ordained, not because they are a different kind of Christian by virtue of the office, but because they are called by God and ordained by the church (here my theological biases are showing) to a special assignment within the church.

These relationships of clergy and laity in ministry provide a highly suggestive model for analyzing their relationships in continuing education. In education for their joint ministries, it is often appropriate that they participate in educational events together as coequals. Sometimes, laity will appropriately be engaged without clergy, or with clergy as teachers, in relation to their unique ministry. Finally, the clergy will often be engaged without laity, or with laity as teachers, here also in relation to their unique ministry.

Obviously, the model for educational relationships will not always follow the model for relationships in ministry. But the analogy is useful.

In this as in other matters intransigent reality factors intervene to modify the ideal. Clergy and laity spend much of their working lives on different time schedules and separated physically. If continuing education is to be construed as broadly as I have defined it, it is not always possible for clergy and laity to participate together even when it would be desirable.

CONTINUING EDUCATION ESPECIALLY
FOR THE LAITY

Education for laity in the church is a large and complex concern, not the primary concern of this book, though it will be touched on in this chapter. Let me therefore mention here only one matter which relates closely to the above model for ministry. It has always been important, but today it is crucial that laity learn how to minister in and to the structures outside the church. In some cases, they and the clergy can engage in this task as co-learners. There are many occasions, however, when it is appropriate for laity to learn as laity, with clergy or other church professionals as teachers.

Several years ago I spent a memorable evening in the North Haven United Methodist Church in Dallas, Texas, while the Rev. William A. Holmes was pastor.[7] Approximately forty persons of all ages were engaged in a study of the power structures of Dallas and the imperatives of the faith for ministering to them as lay persons. That particular evening they were studying the concepts and uses of power in the Old Testament with Bill Holmes as teacher. Soon they would study a master's thesis which analyzed the power structures of Dallas. At the end each would choose one way to relate to these structures, and the group would then meet monthly to discuss their various involvements.

CONTINUING EDUCATION ESPECIALLY FOR THE CLERGY

Similarly, there are ministries distinctive to professional leaders, which indicate education separately from the laity. In training, for example, for various skills—preaching, teaching, worship leadership, counseling—to ask lay persons to always be involved as partners would be cumbersome if not senseless. I as a layman in medicine have no desire to learn how to perform any operation or prescribe medicine. It would be a waste of my time to go with a surgeon or my family doctor to

[7] For a description of the basic congregational study program called the "Community Dialogue," cf. William A. Holmes, *Tomorrow's Church: A Cosmopolitan Community* (Nashville: Abingdon Press, 1968), especially pp. 87-104.

learn such a thing. It is just as silly to argue that lay persons should be partners with clergy in all education programs.

This is not to say that education relative to our distinctive function would not be enriched by involvement of lay persons, not primarily as fellow students, but as teachers and resource persons. For many years the weekend clinics on communication in preaching were one of the most effective elements in the seminars led by Dr. Reuel Howe at the Institute for Advanced Pastoral Studies. Following a Sunday morning service a selected group of lay persons would reflect on what they had heard in the sermon while the seminar participants did the same. In the evening the two groups met to share their perceptions. Many times the differences in what the two groups had heard were startling.

The laity, I am sure, learned significantly from these discussions, but their role in the event was not primarily as fellow student but as resource persons to the seminar participants as they addressed the problem of communication through preaching.

Whether lay persons are physically present or not, they can never be out of mind. The serious weakness of much continuing education for clergy does not inhere in the laity's physical absence. In some highly effective programs using a clinical case method, they are almost never present. The weakness occurs, rather, when their concerns, their viewpoints, and needs are left out of account.

CLERGY AND LAITY TOGETHER IN CONTINUING EDUCATION

To reaffirm what has been already said, in the ministry of the whole People of God, ministries of clergy and laity overlap in a larger area than they are distinct. *The claim, then, cannot be too strongly made that in these areas learning will be much more ecumenical (whole) when the ordained and unordained*

*ministers in the church learn together. Each has much to con-
tribute to the other, and they need the mutual base in learning
as they move in koinonia (genuine commonality) into ministry
in the world.*

Many instances can be cited in which this claim is borne out.
Several years ago a United Methodist seminary conducted a
course in theology for a group of lay persons and their pastors.
Enrollment was accepted only by teams of two lay persons and
one pastor from a church. Each Monday evening for one semester these groups drove as much as one hundred miles to participate. The leaders reported that several sessions were required
before the barriers between laity and clergy began to dissolve.
The pastors had difficulty—as some finally confessed—in relinquishing to the laity their presumed monopoly of religious
knowledge. Gradually, however, it became apparent that the
clergy were enriching the study because of their theological
knowledge and the laity because of their knowledge of what
it is like in the world to the great value of the total enterprise.

One of the most hopeful signs in the church today is the
renewal of congregations through the help of skilled consultants.
The Center for Parish Development and Project Test Pattern
are only two of such consulting agencies.[8] A primary key to
the effectiveness of this process is apparently the engagement of
pastors (and other professional leaders) and the congregation
together in a goal setting-planning-learning endeavor.

Until recently I was a member of an experimental inter-
agency team which served as consultants to a parish in the upper
Midwest. We watched some remarkable changes occur in this
medium-sized ex-urban parish, partially through long-range
educative processes. The pastor and lay persons recognized their
distinctive roles in the congregation. But more often than not

[8] For an especially good description of parish consultations, cf. Loren B.
Mead, *New Hope for Congregations* and Elias L. Desportes, *Congregations
in Change* (New York: The Seabury Press, 1972 and 1973). Study guides
are available for each of these books.

their identities merged as they worked together on processes which they hoped would make for renewal in mission.

The need for effective human relationships is certainly not unique to clergy or laity. Training a church professional in human relations without the presence of lay persons should be the exception. Involvement with laity, as well as with persons outside the church, will not only sharpen communication skills more effectively but will often build understandings of the laity (and of the clergy by the laity) which will be useful long after the training event in narrowing the clergy-laity gap.

The illustrations could continue, but most of you have yourself experienced values of being co-learners with laity. The important thing is for us to begin imaginatively to create occasions in our own congregations in which we are co-learners with laity and to plan our continuing education programs so that, when appropriate, we engage lay persons as colleagues.

The remainder of this chapter is devoted to two specific matters which fit most naturally here because they focus on particular aspects of clergy-lay relationships.

CHIEF TEACHER IN THE CONGREGATION

A pastor or Christian educator is a chief teacher in the congregation. This is a bold claim, but I believe it is valid and can be sustained. If so, it has substantial bearing on continuing education.

The foundation of the claim is that the congregation is the school of the church. The church maintains other schools to carry out specialized tasks, but the vast proportion of the laity will be educated in the congregation, or not at all, insofar as matters of the faith are concerned.

Responsibility for this education will be carried to a great extent by the laity themselves. That is exactly as it should be. But if we seriously believe that the congregation is the school of the church, a major teaching role remains which can be carried only by the church's professional leadership.

163

Solid grounding in our tradition undergirds the chief teacher role. Relative to the gospel the early church recognized two primary functions: proclamation or *kerygma* and teaching or *didache.* The four Gospels contain both: Mark exemplifies primarily *kerygma;* Matthew, *didache.* The Teaching of the Twelve Apostles (*The Didache*) is an early noncanonical book which symbolizes the great importance of the teaching function.

In recent years, however, *kerygma* has far outshone *didache* in the image of the pastor. Witness the popular appellation "preacher" for the pastor's role. (How many times have you been called "teacher" in public?) The Christian educator has been seen as one who keeps the church school going and trains teachers on occasion, but only seldom as a chief teacher in the congregation.

But winds of change are blowing. Here and there teaching ministers are now employed on church staffs or in group ministries. In some instances where the title is not used, it is assumed that one major function in a staff is the teaching role. More significant, perhaps, is the growing number of pastors and Christian educators who have decided that the congregation is indeed the school of the church and that they will teach as a primary role. *Didache* is, I believe, recovering its historic place.

Why? Two reasons stand out: 1) the new cultural situation in which apologetics is again crucial; 2) new concepts of education.

1) Apologetics is now essential. We are again in an age when we cannot take it for granted that almost everyone wants to be Christian, or even understands what it would mean. Neither can we assume that everyone who is Christian realizes the demands of being faithful (this has been true in every era).

In this situation the task of convincing and interpreting—the task of apologetics—is demanding. The task cannot be accomplished without effective teaching—teaching which reflects knowledge of the tradition, knowledge of the contemporary world, an open mind, and skill in the teaching process itself.

2) The second reason for the recovery of *didache* is renewed awareness of education's power as a change agent. Change, growth, and education are becoming interlocking concepts. To claim that something is happening now which has not happened before is always risky. That education creates sheer cognitive change has never been questioned; common sense knows that. And I suppose that the great educators have always known that learning creates profound change. Now, however, there is a renewed conviction that education changes the way we function, the way we act; it is food for growth.

For many generations, the church has professed that fundamental change—the change that really matters—comes through some kind of religious experience: participation in the sacraments, mystical experience, conversion. Once that happens, education can interpret the experience, confirm it, more fully ground it. Education, after all, is of the head; real change is of the heart. This may be overdrawn, but it comes close to the commonly held view, especially that of the average church member. This view must now be reassessed.

John Dewey began the revolution in American society which has moved constantly toward the linkage of change and education. No movement of this sort is without excesses and shallow claims. One could get the impression that education is nothing more than growth and that everything which produces growth is education. The fact remains, however, that many now realize that education can and does produce profound change, especially when it deals with feelings as well as ideas.

John Gardner is a major proponent of education as a change agent. His book *Self-Renewal* in its entirety is testimony to the idea. He says:

We are beginning to understand how to educate for renewal but we must deepen that understanding. If we indoctrinate the young person in an elaborate set of fixed beliefs, we are ensuring his early obsolescence. The alternative is to develop skills, attitudes, habits of mind and the kinds of knowledge and understanding that will be the instruments of continuous change and growth on the part of the young person. Then we will have fashioned *a system that provides for its own continuous renewal.*[9]

All of this is not to disclaim the power of religious experience as a change agent. It is to say, however, that the church must now recognize that education is also a powerful change agent, that *didache* has its place alongside *kerygma,* not beneath or beyond it.

What is involved when one accepts the role of chief teacher in the congregation? Certainly not being the sole teacher or even excluding laity from heavy and significant teaching roles.

I referred above to the community dialogue program of North Haven Church. The foundation of this program has been a basic course in which hundreds of the members of the congregation have been involved. In the beginning the pastor taught the course. Gradually, however, lay persons were identified who showed potential as its teachers. The pastor began to work with them. They were finally recognized by the congregation as lay theologians and took over the teaching of the basic course while the pastor taught the advanced courses and continued to consult with them.

This is a good illustration of the chief teacher role of preparing others to assume major teaching responsibility. But it is only one of many, the most obvious of which is the training of church school teachers.

The role is carried out also in the use of the sermon as an opportunity for *didache* as well as *kerygma;* in discovery and use of teaching opportunities in a variety of tasks such as counseling, visiting, administration, meetings. One pastor whom

[9] John W. Gardner, *Self-Renewal: The Individual in the Innovative Society* (New York: Harper & Row, 1965), p. 21.

I know has developed short courses of study for persons confined to the hospital. The opportunities are myriad.

When the variety of opportunities are recognized, it remains to be said that direct teaching of the laity to equip them in the faith and for their mission in the world is the primary task. The incident at North Haven described earlier is a good example. More and more pastors tell me that they are teaching special courses constantly throughout the year. Preparatory membership classes are being taken more seriously. A friend of mine conducts an eight-month weekly course for youth preparing for confirmation and says it is one of his most satisfying and productive activities.

Being a chief teacher in the congregation has two direct implications for continuing education: 1) Most of us need further training as teachers, especially skill in effective adult education. Few programs exist designed especially for church professionals, but many of us live near colleges and universities where courses in adult education are offered.

2) Some of our most effective learning will occur as we prepare to teach others. If we take the role seriously, we will teach in a wide variety of subject areas over a period of time. Our learning will have residual values far beyond its immediate use. We will also discover areas of interest and competence which will provide opportunity for specialization.

THE MULTIPLE STAFF

Thousands of churches have professional staffs of three or more persons. Many include both clergy and laity and thus represent in a special way the larger issue of this chapter. One encounters heartening examples of team relationships in which members are mutually supportive. Many staffs see themselves as learning groups and thus become a significant locus for continuing education.

Unhappily, however, these are the exception. More often staff members see one another as more threatening than supportive.

Hostilities are either pushed back or destructively expressed. Work is hindered, not helped, and the only learning is that one's fellow professional in ministry is the enemy.

A major source of data comes from directors and ministers of Christian education. The problem was forcefully brought to my attention at a national meeting of Christian educators in 1966. For several days I listened to discussions of the problems and issues which they faced in their work. Over and over, the major problem stated had to do with staff relationships. At times strong, pent-up hostility was evident. Since that meeting I have discussed this problem with numerous persons and have found my initial impressions confirmed. The Reverend R. Harold Hipps, Executive Officer of the Christian Educators Fellowship,[10] says that staff relationships rank as one of the several most critical problems for professionals in this field all over the United States. The Waldrep Study (see p. 155) ranks staff relationships as the second most frequently reported problem.

The Christian educator, church administrator, or director of music who is a lay person is often treated as a second-rate employee because of that fact. The problem is too often reported by competent individuals to be shunted aside.

Mr. Hipps and others strongly advocate that the answer to the problem lies partly in upgrading basic educational standards for lay church professionals. One may be treated as less than competent because that is the fact. A good case can be made for Christian educators, administrators, and musicians having graduate professional degrees. But basic education is not our primary concern here.

For staffs where problems now exist, continuing education may offer a way to resolve the problem. Beyond that, it offers to all staffs—denominational agencies and others—a means to enhance their work individually and together.

---

[10] Mr. Hipps is Associate General Secretary of the Division of Lay Ministries, United Methodist Board of Higher Education and Ministry.

Now in increasing numbers, seminars and workshops are being planned especially to enhance staff relationships. The most effective appear to be those in which staffs engage together. In the absence of program offerings, nothing is to prevent a staff from taking its own initiative. It could also join with several staffs in the same city to plan a program and engage their own resource persons. Better still, a staff can find a consultant to sit with it in regular staff meetings. In this way the actual situation becomes immediate data for learning.

The multiple staff is an excellent colleague learning group. The study guides and other resources referred to in chapter 5 are being used increasingly by staffs. Several years ago the church which I attend invited the laity to study the Sermon on the Mount at breakfast meetings during Lent. The study was different from many in that a minister and a lay person led the sessions jointly after they had grappled with the meaning of a passage. As advance preparation each week the church staff studied the passages, first working exegetically on the meaning and then testing their own understanding of what it required in life. They reported that this had value for them far beyond the immediate preparation for work with the lay group.[11]

Eight years ago I had just begun my work in continuing education for ministry. About that time a former colleague took a job related to continuing education for the laity. A few months later he said to me, "Neither of us is primarily concerned with education for clergy or laity. We are both engaged, from different perspectives, in the education of the church for its life and mission." My friend's words made a lasting impression.

My work since, and this book, have focused primarily on continuing education for professional leaders in the church. The hope has remained, however, that it will finally be education which will equip the church—the whole church.

---

[11] An unpublished study of multiple staffs in 1972 revealed that one of the primary needs for joint study was felt in the biblical and theological area.

EPILOGUE
AS PARABLE

William Muehl tells this story in *all the damned angels*.[1]

"Early in the last century, in the days when the great fleet of sailing ships went out of New Bedford to scour the oceans of the world for whale oil, the most famous skipper of them all was Eleazar Hull. Captain Hull took his vessel into more remote seas, brought home greater quantities of oil, and lost fewer crewmen in the process than any other master of his time. And all this was the more remarkable, because he had no formal navigational training of any kind. When asked how he guided his ship infallibly over the desert of waters he would reply, 'Well, I go up on deck, listen to the wind in the riggin', get the drift of the sea, and take a long look at the stars. Then I set my course.'

"One day, however, the march of time caught up with this ancient mariner. The insurance company whose agents covered the ships of Captain Hull's employers declared that they would no longer write a policy for any ship whose master did not meet certain formal standards of education in the science of

[1] (Philadelphia: Pilgrim Press, 1972), p. 16.

navigation. Captain Hull's superiors could understand this new rule. But they were at a loss to know how to approach the proud man whose life had been spent on the bridge and tell him that he must eigher go back to school or retire. After some consultation they decided to meet the problem head on. Three of the company's top executives waited on Captain Hull and put their dilemma as tactfully as possible.

"To their amazement the old fellow responded enthusiastically. He had, it appeared, always wanted to know something about "science," and he was entirely willing to spend several months studying it. So arrangements were made. Eleazar Hull went to school, studied hard, and graduated near the top of his class. Then he returned to his ship, set out to sea, and was gone for two years.

"When the skipper's friends heard that he was putting into port again, they met him in an informal delegation at the docks. They enquired eagerly how it felt to navigate by the book after so many years of doing it the other way.

" 'It was wonderful,' Captain Hull responded. 'Whenever I wanted to know my position, I'd go to my cabin, get out all the charts, work through the proper equations, and set a course with mathematical precision. Then I'd go up on deck, get the drift of the sea, listen to the wind in the riggin', and take a long look at the stars. And correct my computations for error.' "

Eleazar, by the way, when translated means "God has helped."

BIBLIOGRAPHY

Adams, Henry. "Effectiveness in Ministry: A Proposal for Lay-Clergy Collegiality." *The Christian Ministry,* January, 1971.

Back, Kurt W. "The Group Can Comfort but Can't Cure." *Psychology Today* 6 (December, 1972).

Bentley (Doely), Sarah. *Women: Perspectives on a Movement.* Pittsburgh: Thesis Educational Resources, 1973.

_____ *Women: Over Half the Earth's People.* Pittsburgh: Thesis Educational Resources, 1973.

Biersdorf, John E., ed. *Ministry in the Seventies.* New York: IDOC-NA, 1971.

Blue Book, The. Part III. Report to the 181st General Assembly of The United Presbyterian Church in the U.S.A., 1969.

Book of Discipline of The United Methodist Church, The. Nashville: The United Methodist Publishing House, 1972.

Brown, Thomas E. "The Search for Vocation in Middle Life." *Eastern Career Development Newsletter* Vol. I, No. 1.

Clausen, John A., ed. *Socialization and Society.* Boston: Little, Brown, 1968.

"Competence in the Parish Ministry." *Journal of the Academy of Parish Clergy* 3, May 1973.

Drucker, Peter F. *The Effective Executive.* New York: Harper & Row, 1967.

_____. "The University in an Educated Society." *The Oakland Papers,* James B. Whipple and Cary A. Woditsch, eds. Boston: Center for the Study of Liberal Education for Adults, 1966.

Erikson, Erik H. *Childhood and Society.* 2nd ed. New York: W. W. Norton & Co., 1963.

Fried, Barbara. "The Middle-Age Crisis." *McCall's Magazine,* March, 1967.

Gamble, Connolly. "The Continuing Education of the Minister." In *Proceedings, 1966 Navy Supervisory Chaplains Conference.* Washington: Bureau of Naval Personnel: Chaplains Division, 1966.

————. "Short-Term Programs of Continuing Education." In *The Continuing Quest*, James B. Hofrenning, ed. Minneapolis: Augsburg Press, 1970.

Gardner, John W. *Self-Renewal: The Individual in the Innovative Society.* New York: Harper & Row, 1965.

Gilkey, Langdon Brown. *Naming the Whirlwind.* Indianapolis: Bobbs-Merrill, 1969.

Ginsburg, Herbert, and Opper, Sylvia. *Piaget's Theory of Intellectual Development: An Introduction.* Englewood Cliffs, N.J.: Prentice-Hall, 1969.

Glasse, James D. *Profession: Ministry.* Nashville: Abingdon Press, 1968.

————. *Putting It Together in the Parish.* Nashville: Abingdon Press, 1973.

Hadden, Jeffrey K. *The Gathering Storm in the Churches.* Garden City, N.Y.: Doubleday & Co., 1969.

————."The Gathering Storm Revisited." *Journal* (United Church of Christ) 1 (Spring, 1972).

Harris, Thomas A. *I'm OK, You're OK.* New York: Harper & Row, 1969.

Harvey, Van A. "On Separating Hopes from Illusions." *motive,* November, 1965.

Heston, Warner R., Jr. "Occupational Role Differentiation in Early Career Development of The Protestant Parish Ministry." Ph.D. dissertation, North Carolina State University, 1973.

Holmes, Urban I., III. *The Future Shape of Ministry.* New York: The Seabury Press, 1971.

Holmes, William A. *Tomorrow's Church: A Cosmopolitan Community.* Nashville: Abingdon Press, 1968.

Howe, Reuel L. "The Continuing Education Needs of the Church's Ministry." *Consultation on Continuing Education for the Ministry* (Consultation Proceedings), Ralph E. Peterson, ed. New York: National Council of Churches of Christ in the U.S.A., Department of Ministry, 1964.

Hughes, Everett C. "The Professions in Society." *The Canadian Journal of Economics and Political Science* 26 (February, 1964).

James, Muriel, and Jongeward, Dorothy. *Born to Win: Transactional Analysis with Gestalt Experiments.* Reading, Mass.: Addison-Wesley Publishing Co., 1971.

Jones, O. William. *Sunday Night at the Movies.* Richmond: John Knox Press, 1967.

Kallen, Horace M. "The Continuing Task." CSLEA Pamphlet No. 54.

Bibliography

Marney, Carlyle. "Interpreters' House: A Way Station for Understanding." *Thesis Theological Cassettes,* Vol. 3, No. 2.

Marty, Martin, ed. *Context: A Commentary on the Interaction of Religion and Culture.* Thomas More Association.

Mead, Loren B. "Measuring Ministries." *The Christian Ministry,* January, 1973.

————. *New Hope for Congregations.* New York: The Seabury Press, 1972.

Mills, Edgar W. *Peer Groups and Professional Development: Evaluation Report of the Young Pastors Pilot Project.* Nashville: United Methodist Board of Higher Education, 1973.

Mills, Edgar W., and Kovall, John P. *Stress in the Ministry.* Washington, D.C.: Ministry Studies Board, 1971.

Neugarten, Bernice L., ed. *Middle-Age and Aging.* Chicago: University of Chicago Press, 1968.

NTL Institute News and Reports, Vol. 2, No. 2, April, 1968.

O'Connor, Elizabeth. *Journey Inward, Journey Outward.* New York: Harper & Row, 1968.

Oden, Thomas C. *The Intensive Group Experience.* Philadelphia: Westminster Press, 1972.

Ogg, Elizabeth. *Sensitivity Training and Encounter Groups.* Public Affairs Committee, 1972.

Perls, Frederick S. *Gestalt Therapy Verbatim.* New York: Bantam Books, 1969.

Plan of Union for the Church of Christ Uniting, A. Princeton, N.J.: Consultation on Church Union, 1970.

Prince, George. *The Practice of Creativity.* New York: Harper & Row, 1970.

Reber, Robert E. "The World Council of Churches and World Development: Proposals for Adult Education in the Churches." Ph.D. dissertation, Boston University, 1973.

"Report on Grailville." New York: Church Women United, 1972.

Rouch, Mark A., ed. *Proceedings of the Consultation on Continuing Education for Ministers of The United Methodist Church.* Nashville: United Methodist Board of Education, Division of Higher Education, Department of the Ministry, 1968.

Smith, Donald P. *Clergy in the Cross Fire* (Philadelphia: Westminster Press, 1973).

Smith, Huston. "Education in a Changing World," *Consultation on Continuing Education for the Ministry* (Consultation Proceedings), Ralph E. Peterson, ed. New York: National Council of Churches of Christ in the U.S.A., Department of Ministry, 1946.

Super, Donald E. "Career Development: Life Stages, Developmental Tasks, and Individual Differences." In *The Church and Its Manpower Management,* Ross P. Scherer and Theodore O. Wedel, eds. New

York: National Council of Churches of Christ in the U.S.A., 1966
_____. *The Psychology of Careers.* New York: Harper & Brother ,
1957.

Toffler, Alvin M. *Future Shock.* New York: Random House, 1970.

Tough, Allen M. *The Adult's Learning Projects.* Toronto: Institute for
Studies in Education, 1971.

Waldrep, Elizabeth Anne. "How Satisfied are Women Professionals in
the Church?" *Professionally Yours.* Nashville: Christian Educators
Fellowship, The United Methodist Church, Summer 1973.

White, Robert W. *Lives in Progress: A Study of the Natural Growth of
Personality.* New York: Holt, Rinehart and Winston, 1952.

Winter, J. Alan; Mills, Edgar W.; *et al. Clergy in Action Training:
A Research Report.* New York: IDOC and the Ministry Studies
Board, 1971.

APPENDIX I

AGENCIES RELATED TO CONTINUING EDUCATION
FOR MINISTRY

Academy of Parish Clergy, 3100 West Lake Street, Minneapolis, Minnesota 55416.

Action-Training Coalition, c/o M.E.T.C. (one of the Action-Training agencies), 1419 V Street, NW, Washington, D.C. 20009.

Adult Education Association, The Otis Building, 810 18th Street, NW, Washington, D.C. 20006.

Association of Clinical Pastoral Education, 475 Riverside Drive, Suite 450, New York, New York 10027.

Career Development Council, 475 Riverside Drive, Room 760, New York, New York 10027.

Christian Educators Fellowship, P.O. Box 871, Nashville, Tennessee 37202.

Committee on Continuing Education for Clergy Land Grant Colleges and State Universities, c/o Division of Community Resource Development, Federal Extension Service, U.S. Department of Agriculture, Washington, D.C. 20250.

Interfaith Council for Family Financial Planning, 1701 K Street, NW, Suite 1001, Washington, D.C. 20006.

National Council of Churches of Christ in the U.S.A., Committee on Professional Leadership, 475 Riverside Drive, New York, New York 10027.

National Institute for Applied Behavioral Science, 1201 Sixteenth Street, NW, Washington, D.C. 20036.

Society for the Advancement of Continuing Education for Ministry, 3401 Brook Road, Richmond, Virginia 23227.

DENOMINATIONAL OFFICES RELATED TO CONTINUING EDUCATION

The offices listed are primary contacts for continuing education information related to a particular denomination. Only that part of the agency title which is necessary as a mailing address is listed in most cases. Especially in large denominations, more than one agency is related to continuing education. Those listed, however, can put the enquirer in touch with the appropriate agency.

American Baptist Convention, Educational Ministries, Valley Forge, Pennsylvania 19481.

The American Lutheran Church, Division of Theological Education and Ministry, 422 South Fifth Street, Minneapolis, Minnesota 55415.

The Anglican Church of Canada, Consultant for Continuing Education, 600 Jarvis Street, Toronto, Ontario M4Y2J6.

Christian Church (Disciples of Christ), Department of Ministry and Worship, 222 South Downey Avenue, Indianapolis, Indiana 46219.

Church of the Brethren, General Office, 1451 Dundee Avenue, Elgin, Illinois 60120.

Church of the Nazarene, Department of Education and Ministry, 6401 The Paseo, Kansas City, Missouri 64131.

The Episcopal Church, Board for Theological Education, 935 East Avenue, Rochester, New York 14607.

Friends United Meeting, Meeting Ministries Commission, 101 Quaker Hill Drive, Richmond, Indiana 47374.

The Lutheran Church—Missouri Synod, Board for Higher Education, 500 North Broadway, St. Louis, Missouri 63102.

Mennonite Church, The General Conference, Division of Ministry and Personnel, Box 347, Newton, Kansas 67114.

Presbyterian Church in Canada, Personnel Services, 50 Wynford Drive, Don Mills, Ontario.

Presbyterian Church, U.S., Office of Continuing Education and Institutional Relations, 341 Ponce de Leon Avenue, NE, Atlanta, Georgia 30308.

Reformed Church in America, Office of Human Resources, 475 Riverside Drive, New York, New York 10027.

The Roman Catholic Church, Office of Priestly Formation, 1312 Massachusetts Avenue, NW, Washington, D.C. 20005.

Southern Bapist Convention, Seminary Extension Department, 460 James Robertson Parkway, Nashville, Tennessee 37219.

Unitarian Universalist Association, Department of the Ministry, 25 Beacon Street, Boston, Massachusetts 02108.

United Church of Canada, Division of the Ministry, 85 St. Clair Avenue, East, Toronto 7, Ontario.

United Church of Christ, Office of Church Life and Leadership, 287 Park Avenue, South, New York, New York 10010.

The United Methodist Church, Division of the Ordained Ministry, P.O. Box 871, Nashville, Tennessee 37202.

The United Presbyterian Church, U.S.A., Vocation Agency, 475 Riverside Drive, New York, New York 10027.

APPENDIX II

A SAMPLE CASE STUDY

This case study was published in Christian Ministry, March, 1973, *supplied by the Case Study Project of Lancaster Theological Seminary.*

BACKGROUND: John is sixteen years old, the second of four children in a family which is active in our congregation. He exhibits more than average intelligence and sensitivity to himself and others. His youngest brother, Richard, has a brain disease, and nearly died three years ago. He requires constant and very delicate medication to control spasm and outbursts of anxiety. The family experiences considerable stress as a result of this illness and related financial problems.

In late November, I heard from others that John was planning to run away from home. He showed evidence of depression—sad eyes, listless body. Several soft attempts to open him up had failed. After an evening meeting of young people the first week in December, I invited him to my office. I told him I had heard of his plans to run away. He confirmed this and shared several reasons for his unhappiness. Our conversation indicated that he was not adequately communicating his feelings to his family about matters which troubled him. Our session closed with my encouragement that he initiate communication with his family. We scheduled another session later in the week. At that session, he indicated a start in communication, the resolution of two of the problems he had mentioned, and a general improvement in his mood.

I again urged him to work at communicating his anger and sharing his internal conflicts with members of his family when conflicts arose.

The week after Christmas his mother called to say that he and a friend had run away in John's car. I went to the home and spent most of the morning with the parents discussing the problem. Word came that the boy had been found ninety miles from home, and arrangements were made to return him. I took Richard to our home while the family was gone.

DESCRIPTION: Three days later, I went to the home unannounced at 12:30 P.M. My objective was to determine the family situation and to facilitate communication if that were needed. When I entered, the family was completing a meal in the kitchen. I said hello to John. He got up and went to his room. His mother said she had been crying again. I asked her if they had made any progress since John's return. She said no. I said I would like to talk to John. She went to get him. He returned, she did not. He sat down, seemed uninterested in talking. I moved across the room to a seat next to him. He responded to several questions about his feelings, indicating again that he was not communicating with his family. I asked him if we could discuss this with his mother. When she came in, she discussed in tears John's need to get along better with Richard and to get a job. She indicated that she would do whatever was necessary to make John happy. She discussed her own fatigue and the frustrations of her family. John responded throughout by indicating his love for his family and his confusion about his feelings. I affirmed the strengths of the family and suggested three alternatives for developing communications—psychiatric counseling, counseling with me, or structured family communications sessions. They made no commitment to any of these suggestions. I left with the comment, "I don't want to pry into your family, but I am concerned about you, and I hope that you begin to work out your problems."

A week later, the mother called to say that John had run away in his car with four other teen-agers.

ANALYSIS: This family, like many in our lower middle-class community, has difficulty handling stress. They lack communication skills. The father's role is very nebulous in the family. I experienced anxiety throughout due to role confusion. I felt like an intruder, I wanted to be a counselor. Information from the police indicates an epidemic of runaways. I see a considerable subculture influence in this situation.

EVALUATION: I do not feel that I effectively increased communication within the family because John later ran away. My own uneasiness about my role during a house call contributed to my ineffectiveness. The hesitance of John and his mother to talk with me or with each other added to my uneasiness.

1. How do I define my role in a situation where my presence and help are not sought?

2. What were some alternatives for my intervention in this situation?

3. How do families and others measure and deal with the subculture pressures which influence adolescent children?

INDEX

Kerygma, 164
Koval, John P., 112

Lancaster Theological Seminary,
145-46
Learning needs
assessment of, 55-56, 59, 64, 68,
146-47
Lengrand, Paul, 24
Libraries, 73-74, 75, 130
Lifelong learning
definition, 23, 24, 29
episodes, 22
nondiscipline, 28-29
Lowe, John C., 125
Lutheran Church in America, 97

Maheu, Rene, 24
Marcion, 44
Marney, Carlyle, 43, 83
Marty, Martin E., 45, 74
M.A.S.H., 41
Masland Fellows, 98
Mead, Loren, 146, 162
Mead, Margaret, 14
Menninger Foundation, 89
Merrill Fellows, 20, 98
Middlesence, 122
Mills, Edgar W., 87, 100, 112
Mind as resource, 71
Moore, Joan W., 125
Muehl, William, 171
Multiple staffs, 164, 167-69
Murray, Richard, 45, 76

National Training Laboratories, 85
Neugarten, Bernice, 119, 122, 123
New Dimensions, 76

New York Theological Seminary,
83

O'Connor, Elizabeth, 50
Oden, Thomas C., 86
Ogg, Elizabeth, 85
Oppenheimer, Robert, 37
Opper, Sylvia, 39

Pagett, Betty Strathman, 89, 90
Parish, 14-15, 162
Parish Ministers Fellowship, 97
Perkins School of Theology, 76,
143, 148
Perls, Frederick S., 25
Personal growth
evaluation, 64-65
primary processes, 54, 118, 131,
135-37
professional practice, 53-54
programs for, 84-86
Piaget, Jean, 39
Peterson, Ralph E., 158
Plan for Continuing Education
compromise, 61
flexibility, 61
key to continuing education, 60
length, 60
majors, 61-62
minors, 61-62
sample plan, 63-64
Planning
basic questions, 53-58
a case study, 51-53
clergy-laity relationships, 153,
159-69
counsel for, 50, 60, 98-99
importance, 60